BUDDENBROOKS

*Family Life as the
Mirror of Social Change*

TWAYNE'S MASTERWORK STUDIES

Robert Lecker, General Editor

BUDDENBROOKS

Family Life as the
Mirror of Social Change

MARTIN SWALES

TWAYNE PUBLISHERS • BOSTON
A Division of G. K. Hall & Co.

Twayne's Masterwork Studies No. 7 9

Copyright 1991 by G. K. Hall & Co.
All rights reserved.
Published by Twayne Publishers
A division of G. K. Hall & Co.
70 Lincoln Street
Boston, Massachusetts 02111

Copyediting supervised by Barbara Sutton.
Book production by Janet Z. Reynolds.
Typeset by Compset, Inc., Beverly, Massachusetts.

10 9 8 7 6 5 4 3 2 1 (hc)
10 9 8 7 6 5 4 3 2 1 (pb)

The paper used in this publication meets the minimum requirements
of American National Standard for Information Sciences—Permanence
of Paper for Printed Library Materials, ANSI Z39.48-1984. ⊚™

Printed and bound in the United States of America.

Library of Congress Cataloging-in-Publication Data
Swales, Martin.
    Buddenbrooks : family life as the mirror of social change / Martin
Swales.
        p.   cm.—(Twayne's masterwork studies : no. 79)
    Includes bibliographical references and index.
    ISBN 0-8057-9402-6. — ISBN 0-8057-8551-5 (pbk.)
    1. Mann, Thomas, 1875–1955. Buddenbrooks.   2. Family in literature.
    3. Mann, Thomas, 1875–1955—Political and social views.
    I. Mann, Thomas, 1875–1955. Buddenbrooks. II. Title. III. Series.
    PT2625.A44B92 1991
833'.912—dc20   91–13065
                                                                              CIP

For
Hansjörg and Kate Meyer

CONTENTS

Thomas Mann, around 1900. *Courtesy of the Thomas Mann Archive, Zurich.*

NOTE ON THE REFERENCES
AND ACKNOWLEDGMENTS

Quotations from *Buddenbrooks* are given in parentheses, with part numbers in Roman numerals and chapter numbers in Arabic. Thus readers will be able to find the particular quotation regardless of the edition they possess. All translations are my own, quite simply because I felt that my argument frequently calls for a closer, word-for-word rendering of the German text than any professional translator can or should provide. However, because of the wide dissemination of Helen T. Lowe-Porter's translation in the Vintage Books paperback edition (New York: Random House, 1961), I have also provided page references to this edition following the parenthetical citation of part and chapter number.

I am grateful to the Thomas Mann Archive of the Eidgenössische Technische Hochschule, Zurich, for providing me with, and for allowing me to reproduce here, one photograph of Thomas Mann around 1900 and another of the "Buddenbrook House" in Lübeck. My thanks go also to the editors of *Modern Language Review* for allowing me to reprint, in chapters 1 and 2, a few paragraphs that first appeared in that journal as part of the article "'Neglecting the Weight of the Elephant . . .': German Prose Fiction and European Realism" (*MLR* 83 [1988]:882–94). In November 1989 I had the privilege of giving a lecture on Thomas Mann under the auspices of the Ida Herz Bequest to the English Goethe Society. That lecture, "Symbolic Patterns or Realistic Plenty? Thomas Mann's *Buddenbrooks* and the European Novel," is to appear in due course in the *Publications of the English Goethe Society*. Parts of the argument—and, on occasion, of the actual text itself—overlap with sections of this volume. I am grateful to both sets of editors for allowing this sharing to occur.

Buddenbrooks was the first novel by Thomas Mann that I came across. I have never forgotten the thrill of that first reading, not least because the thrill is still there on every rereading. Nobody—still less a professional Germanist like myself—reads in a vacuum, and I am well aware that my responses to this great work have been immeasurably modified and enriched by dialogue with other readers. My indebtedness to fellow scholars is indicated in the Notes and Selected Bibliography. I also owe a very great deal to my students at Birmingham, Toronto, and London for those face-to-face debates which are so much the lifeblood of literary studies. My wife, Erika, has discussed the novel with me more times and over more years than either of us cares to remember.

It is, however, a very particular debt of gratitude that I wish to acknowledge in dedicating this study to Hansjörg and Kate Meyer. In my first year as a university teacher (in the German Department of Birmingham University), a young German *Lektor* was also appointed, and we soon became close friends. In part, our friendship derived from a shared delight in imaginative literature, a delight in which each of us felt a particular love for the other's national literature. In matters of literary taste, Hansjörg was and is more Anglophile than I am, and I was and am more Germanophile than he. Perhaps that is why our discussions have been so energetic and absorbing, an excitement that has been compounded by the involvement of his Scots wife, Kate. To them I offer this volume in gratitude and love.

CHRONOLOGY:
THOMAS MANN'S LIFE AND WORKS

1875   On 6 June, Paul Thomas Mann is born in Lübeck, the second
            son of Thomas Johann Heinrich Mann and Julia Mann (née
            da Silva-Bruhns). Lübeck's constitution is incorporated into
            that of the German Empire.

1882   Thomas Mann begins his schooling. His early years coincide
            with ever more dramatic signs of the economic and interna-
            tional self-confidence of the German Empire. The population
            of Berlin soon passes the million mark, and colonial expansion
            is energetically pursued.

1890   Mann firm celebrates centenary in May.

1891   Mann's father, a highly respected grain merchant and senator,
            dies. In his will he decrees the liquidation of the firm, appar-
            ently having realized—with no bitterness or resentment—that
            his two elder sons, Thomas and Heinrich (b. 1871), are set on
            artistic rather than business careers.

1892   Thomas Mann completes his schooling after an undistin-
            guished career as a pupil. He then joins his mother in Munich
            and attends a number of lectures at the university, produces
            some journalism and short stories, and finally enters an insur-
            ance office.

1896–1897   Spends a year in Italy with his brother Heinrich, first in Pales-
            trina, then in Rome. There he receives a letter (dated 29 May
            1897) from Samuel Fischer, the great German publisher, agree-
            ing to publish some of his short prose narratives. Fischer
            states: "I would be very pleased if you would give me the op-
            portunity of publishing a larger prose work by you—perhaps
            a novel."[1] The young author is immensely flattered. He has a
            project that seems to provide the germ of the requested
            novel—a story about a "sensitive latecomer,"[2] a young person
            whose psychological and physical weariness, as the last in the

line of a distinguished family, entails a corresponding endowment with spiritual and imaginative energies. Mann sets about converting the story into a novel by filling in the prehistory of this latecomer.[3] As he does so, he finds himself borrowing extensively from his own family history. From his father's cousin, Wilhelm Marty, he obtains details of public and economic life in Lübeck; from his sister Julia he receives a long account of the life of their Aunt Elisabeth.[4] He incorporates into his novel aspects of his aunt's physical appearance and linguistic behavior as well as details of her emotional life (the love affair while on holiday, the reluctant entering into the first marriage). Aunt Elisabeth becomes Tony Buddenbrook in the novel, but the Tony figure is also based on a character who appears in a contemporary Norwegian novel, *Ein Malstrom* by Jonas Lie.[5]

Mann seems to have the extraordinarily happy knack of coming across facts, details, circumstances, artistic modes and techniques that are grist to his novelistic mill.[6] A cartoon in the satirical magazine *Simplicissimus* suggests to him the outward appearance of Tony's second husband, Permaneder. He owes certain thematic and formal features to his reading of Alexander Kielland, Lie, and the Goncourts (from their novel *Renée Mauperin* he derives the idea of dividing the novel into parts and chapters, thereby allowing for a natural rhythm of short chapters). While perusing the chronicle of his own family, he comes across a motto, first quoted by his grandfather Johann Siegmund Mann as an imperative handed down to him by his father: "My son, work readily by day, but make only such business that we may sleep peacefully at night."[7] Mann slightly modifies this saying and incorporates it into the novel, where it becomes a key motif. Much of the broader sociocultural argument that sustains the novel's overall design is suggested by Georg Brandes's *Die Hauptströmungen der Literatur des 19. Jahrhunderts,* which, incidentally, contains the Turkish proverb quoted by Thomas Buddenbrook: "When the house is ready, death comes."[8] By the time Mann begins work on the novel, he is already familiar with, and profoundly influenced by, Wagner and Nietzsche. Then he suddenly discovers Schopenhauer and reads the philosopher with overwhelming intensity at a time when, in the composition of the novel, he has arrived at the point where Thomas Buddenbrook's life is moving inexorably to its close. The discovery of Schopenhauer comes with the force of a revelation, and the revelation promptly finds its way into the novel.

In October, in Munich, Mann finishes writing his novel,[9]

which has grown in scale beyond anything its young author intended or expected, and sends off to Fischer an unwieldy packet containing the manuscript, handwritten on both sides of the page.

1898   While doing a year's military service—and temporarily in hospital with an inflamed tendon—Mann hears from his publishers, who request that he cut the manuscript by half. He replies instantly with an impassioned defense of the necessity of the novel's length, and Fischer agrees to publish the work as it stands.

1901   First edition of *Buddenbrooks* appears in October in two volumes, a total of 1,100 pages, priced at 12 marks. Sales are relatively sluggish but after a year the first printing of 1,000 copies is exhausted.

1903   Fischer brings out a second edition of *Buddenbrooks* in one volume, costing 5 marks, and the book's success is instant and permanent.

1912   *Death in Venice* published.

1918   World War I ends with the defeat of Germany and the establishment of the Weimar Republic, an attempt to create a modern parliamentary democracy in what had been an imperialist country. Many writers and intellectuals and much of the general public find it difficult to separate the principles of the Weimar Republic from the fact that this government has been imposed on the Germans by their conquerors. Mann's resentment of the Weimar Republic, fueled in part by a bitter feud with his politically progressive brother Heinrich, prompts him to publish an enormous, impassioned, and anguished essay entitled *Reflections of an Unpolitical Man,* which defends the conservative, anti-Western, antidemocratic traditions of Germany as the spiritual homeland of a culture of true inwardness. That spiritual homeland is, so Mann argues, preferable to the liberal, democratic nation state. (Mann subsequently reassesses his understanding of the political consequences of German culture, so that from the early 1920s on he constantly and publicly voices a sophisticated cultural defense of the beleaguered Weimar Republic.)

1924   *The Magic Mountain* published. This novel represents an extraordinarily subtle reckoning with whole areas of the German politicocultural tradition. Conservative Weimar circles have no doubt that the author of the *Reflections of an Unpolitical*

	Man has changed his allegiance, and their resentment is profound.[10]
1927	Mann is awarded the Nobel Prize for literature. The instability of the Weimar Republic intensifies.
1933	Mann leaves Germany on a lecture tour; as the polemical right-wing attacks against him increase, he decides to stay in Switzerland. On 30 January Hitler becomes chancellor and in March issues the Enabling Law, which, by conferring on his government emergency powers in the wake of the Reichstag fire and other civil disturbances, makes him supreme ruler of Germany.
1936	Deprived of his German citizenship, Mann publicly dissociates himself from Hitler's National Socialist regime.
1938	Goes to the United States as a visiting professor at Princeton University and subsequently settles in Pacific Palisades, California.
1939	*Lotte in Weimar* published.
1940	Mann begins broadcasting anti-Nazi speeches on BBC radio.
1943	Completes his sequence of four novels, *Joseph and His Brothers,* which he had begun in 1933.
1947	*Doctor Faustus* published.
1952	Returns to Europe, electing to reside not in either of the German states established after the war but in Switzerland.
1955	Dies 12 August.

*Literary and
Historical Context*

The Buddenbrook House in Lübeck. *Courtesy of the Thomas Mann Archive, Zurich.*

1

The German Background

Thomas Mann is one of the supreme novelists of the twentieth century. By personal and cultural disposition he was attracted to themes having a psychological and philosophical import. *Buddenbrooks,* the most widely read and best loved of Mann's novels, was the result of this attraction: it examines the psychology and philosophy of decadence, art, and reflectivity. But it also explores currents expressive of social and historical conflict and change. Throughout his career Thomas Mann found that all his cherished spiritual and cultural concerns expressed themselves in ways that intimately involved the broader public realm of politics and society. The fastidious psychologist and philosopher becomes the writer who tells stories that amount to the history of his time.

It must not be construed, however, that Mann sought to incorporate historical matter into his fiction in any significant way. None of his major works—*Buddenbrooks* (1901), *Death in Venice* (1912), *The Magic Mountain* (1924), *Doctor Faustus* (1947)—seeks to make a story out of the decisive events of public history. Instead, each reflects and reflects *on* certain key features of the cultural and spiritual temper of the age with which it is concerned; each expresses a profound self-consciousness with respect to the historical implications of its own artistic mode. *Buddenbrooks* is a realistic novel that reflects on the philosophical and cultural implications of literary realism. *Death in Venice* is a novella that reflects on its own finely wrought form as something complicit in the moral and cognitive blindness of its protagonist and of the culture he represents. *The Magic Mountain* is that most German of all novels, a *Bildungsroman;* it explores to what extent the kind of inward, apolitical culture that produces such a novel tradition may also be conducive to political disasters. *Doctor Faustus,* a highly self-conscious montage of aspects of German culture from several centuries, asks whether a concoction of such sophistication, irony, and profound inwardness is not, in certain circumstances, a recipe for political catastrophe.

Although he drew closely on his own family history for *Buddenbrooks,* Mann ultimately produced something far removed from a gossipy soap opera. *Buddenbrooks* is a rich and complex reckoning with a particular way of life. As T. J. Reed has helped us to see,[1] with Mann the family novel became a novel of historical, social, and psychological change. Mann did not use members of the Buddenbrook family as allegorical counters in an overtly sociohistorical scenario; the novel works not at the level of factual accuracy (although there is plenty of that in evidence), not in terms of obviously average, and therefore generalizable, experience, and not, therefore, in terms of one-to-one equivalence. Rather, the conception of history in *Buddenbrooks* relies much more on values and symbols than on facts and events.

Mann found himself reckoning with more than a family legacy in *Buddenbrooks;* his most complex reckoning was with Germany itself. For instance, he was acutely aware of having to debate with three figures who, for him, defined and charted the spiritual landscape of the nineteenth century: Schopenhauer, Wagner, and Nietzsche. As he wrote in his 1918 essay *Reflections of an Unpolitical Man,* "The three names that I find myself invoking when I ask what the bases of my artistic and spiritual education are, and these names are a trinity of eternally linked spirits, a constellation that appears in German skies, but they describe not only profoundly German but also European events, are Schopenhauer, Nietzsche, Wagner."[2] At the time of writing *Buddenbrooks,* Mann's knowledge of Wagner and Nietzsche was much more profound than his familiarity with Schopenhauer. Essentially he knew Schopenhauer as filtered through Wagner and Nietzsche. But his own reading of Schopenhauer coincided with that stage of the novel's composition when he needed to find a moment of spiritual crisis and revelation for Thomas Buddenbrook.

When the short tale of the "sensitive latecomer" was converted into a weighty novel covering four generations of a family, the expansion in scale entailed more than an acquiring of ballast. Rather, the substance of the novel provided the medium for Mann's debate with the world—familial, philosophical, musicological, sociohistorical, literary, cultural, institutional—that had produced him. As so often happens, an artist's reckoning with himself turns out to be an act having much broader implications. As Mann put it in his essay "Lübeck as a Form of Mental and Spiritual Life," "One expresses the most personal matters and is surprised to have touched on national concerns. One expresses the most national of concerns—and lo and behold one has captured the general, the most human of concerns."[3]

No adequate sense of the achievement of *Buddenbrooks* is possible without considering the larger issues that, in one form or another, constantly inform our understanding of the novel's central thematic and stylistic registers. One of these issues is German spiritual identity.

A particularly widespread view of German culture generally admits that it is, in various ways, intelligent, thoughtful, and sophisticated but claims that it is curiously bereft of any sustained relationship with the familiar, empirically knowable, substantial facts of daily living. Instead of concerning themselves vigorously with outward things, the Germans, so the argument runs, attend to such pursuits as music (that supremely nonreferential art), speculative philosophy, and theology (particularly when it assumes the guise of radical inwardness). Of course, even their worst detractors would concede that the Germans have produced a literature of note. But even here, spiritual profundity is still very much the order of the day. German literature, it is said, is hopelessly in love with *Geist,* with the life of the mind, with the inward realm that alone (and here one glimpses the specter of Luther) confers distinction, value, and ultimately, justification. This problematic condition of inwardness reveals its inadequacies nowhere more clearly than in the works of narrative prose that issued from German-speaking countries in the age of European realism—from the mid-eighteenth century onward. Whatever distinction that body of prose writing may have, it is not the distinction of literary realism as commonly defined.

However overstated such a view of German culture may be, there is no doubt an element of truth to it. Certainly German prose literature from Goethe on does pose an acute evaluative problem, and it is all too tempting simply to register the gulf that separates it from the classics of European realism. The dilemma is felt not only by foreign Germanists but also by German critics themselves.[4] German scholars repeatedly stress the artistic mastery of German fiction—its linguistic richness, its sophistication, its symbolic density—only then to admit that, alas, the actual texts feel very spiritual, learned, and rarefied when compared with the achievements of Fielding, Dickens, Stendhal, Balzac, George Eliot, Flaubert, or Tolstoy. The poetry of German narrative fiction derives, so the argument runs, from a mismatch between high literary intelligence and the cruel limitations of the social experience that provides the thematic matter. "Poetic realism" is the artistic transfiguration of backwaterdom. Hence the constant debate in German literary history on the theory of narrative forms: poetry is, throughout the nineteenth century, pitted against prose.[5]

One explanation for the peculiar character of German culture has to do with the political and social history of the German-speaking lands. The argument runs as follows. German literature prior to 1871 was of necessity provincial because before that date Germany did not exist as a national entity in the way other European countries, like France and England, did; that is, as a unified nation state. The "Holy Roman Empire of the German Nation" meant provinces, small territories, in a word, particularism, rather than a cohesive demographic unit whose center of gravity could be found in a capital city. Until the last three decades of the nineteenth century, Germany existed only in its language and culture; it was, to invoke hallowed terms, a cultural and not a political nation, a *Kulturnation* and not a "politische Nation." The social and historical circumstances that encouraged the emergence of the realistic novel in Europe simply did not obtain in the German lands. Hence, to demand European realism of German writers is to demand what, by definition, their culture could not provide.

To this argument we might simply respond that different societies produce different literatures. But matters are not so simple as that, because in much of the thinking about the course of German history and culture there is an often unspoken norm that is invoked. The norm applies both to the history and to the narrative literature, the two phenomena being linked not just by the fact that the historical course of a nation molds its culture but also, more specifically, by the fact that both history and narrative literature have certain presuppositions in common: both involve events linked by a causal chronology.[6]

As far as history is concerned, the norm assumes the following doctrines. The proper course of historical development traced by the modern nation-state entails a gradual process of bourgeois self-assertion in the name of increasing economic power and social mobility. Gradually the middle classes win forms of political influence for themselves by challenging feudal structures and by achieving recognition and representation within an ever more democratic, participatory structure of government. The German lands, it is said, failed to obey this model in the eighteenth and nineteenth centuries; 1830 and 1848 marked dismal failures. Hence, when Germany did finally come into line in 1871, it did so in a condition of curious disequilibrium. By the end of the nineteenth century Germany was a formidable power economically, but was out of step with the times socially and politically. This is the curse of the belated nation, the *verspätete Nation;* this is the time bomb at the heart of, to invoke another canonical term for describing the "special course of German history," the *deutscher Sonderweg.* The upshot is the monstrosity of the Third Reich.

The dangers inherent in such normative historical thinking are manifold; there is, for example, the tendency to absolutize one particular model of historical and political change, to invest historical events—whether of a benign or malignant kind—with the motor force of unexamined and unexplained inevitability. Above all else, there is the danger of ethical stridency: the course of German history becomes the curse.

A cognate, if less hectoring, category of normative thinking is also applied in the argument about the evolution of narrative forms. The tenets can be summarized as follows.[7] The birth of the modern novel is inseparable from the increasing self-assertiveness and self-confidence of the middle class. It expresses a sense of rapid economic change and development. The prevailing ethos derives from the revolutionary energies of capitalism, and the emphasis falls unashamedly on the individual. Timeless norms, inherited doctrines, and traditional paradigms no longer apply. The individual makes his way through the social world as best he can. The points of interaction between the individual self and the palpable, resistant particularities of bourgeois society are manifold: the family, the home, the school, the workhouse, the counting house, the law courts. These points of interaction are points of friction and conflict, and they provide the various stages within the novel's plot sequence.

The bourgeois novel is a narrative form that may be termed realistic precisely because it is concerned with the interplay of the characters' inner, psychological life and the palpable facts *(res)* of society. The novel of European realism is philosophically naive: it is not concerned with asking such philosophical questions as, What is the self? or How do I know that the physical and palpable world is real? Rather, it takes for granted that both inner and outer realms are experienced truths, and are experienced in interaction. It documents the particular forms of interaction that occur at a given time in a given society. The realistic novelist has no doubts that the individual's humanity, or lack of it, can be assessed only with reference to that interplay of inner and outer worlds.

Judged by such norms of realistic fiction, very little German prose shares the assumptions on which the European narrative tradition rests. Many German novels and stories are concerned, so the traditional view suggests, with the inward realm to the virtual exclusion of outward practicalities. German prose constantly raises philosophical issues. Hence—and here the value judgments come in—it is part and parcel of a culture whose enormous intellectual sophistication is all too rarely engaged by or critically concerned with the outer world. Because that culture was powerless to deal with the institutional brutality of the Third Reich, we have the hideous paradox, explored with great eloquence by George Steiner, of camp guards at Auschwitz cherishing Mozart and Hölderlin while continuing with the daily work of exterminating their fellow human beings, This is not to say, of course, that the German novel, on even the most critical of readings, can be held responsible for Auschwitz. Still, it has been seen as implicated in the cast of mind that could do little or nothing to prevent Auschwitz.

These are complex issues. Parts of the orthodox view of the historical and literary *Sonderweg* of Germany ring true, but there are certain features of that view I wish to challenge. At the very least, the notion that the Holy Roman Empire "had to" produce Hitler needs to be questioned. And in regard to the lack of literary realism in German prose, I will draw on certain recent developments in critical and aesthetic theory that demand of us, to put it modestly, a more scrupulous and rigorous examination of the category of literary mimesis than has hitherto been undertaken.

The challenge to the schematic historical view of Germany's cankered development has been mounted very cogently by David Blackbourn and Geoff Eley in their study *The Peculiarities of German History*.[8] They point to the ways in which the historiographic stereotype obscures a number of features of German economic and social life that embody a degree of bourgeois emancipation and enterprise. More important for my purposes is an older study, *German Home Towns* by Mack Walker,[9] which addresses the crucial issue of urban and rural life.

I can best convey Walker's argument by means of the contrast with England—not least because England constitutes that historical and cultural norm of which I have been speaking. In his study *The Country and the City*,[10] Raymond Williams draws attention to the early development of agrarian capitalism in England, which put an end to open-strip farming. In consequence, market towns sprang up to provide the economic infrastructure for the marketing of agrarian production. The functional contrast between country and town was then exacerbated by the Industrial Revolution, which moved the urban community ever farther away from the rhythms of "natural life." All this intensified the nostalgia for a precapitalist, preindustrial, and, above all, preurban world from which large numbers of the population had been banished. It is precisely this sharp disjunction between rural and urban ways of life that did not apply to the German lands, as W. H. Riehl showed in his crucial study *Land und Leute* (for which George Eliot displayed such enthusiasm).[11]

It is vital to notice—and Walker's study helps us in this regard—that the German social consciousness was shaped by the notion of a preindustrial but essentially *urban* culture. In the lands between Prussia to the north and Austria to the south—that is, in the "individualized land" of Riehl's cultural geography—the movement of European trade in the course of the seventeenth and eighteenth centuries toward the north of Europe and the maritime west meant that the "hometowns," such as Ulm, Regensburg, and Nuremberg, became increasingly inward-looking and institutionalized, tied to the relatively stable framework of the guild economy. The skilled master craftsman was the elite figure in an intimate urban world, one sustained not by the economic principles of growth-conscious competition but by custom, convention, familiarity. The great elegy to the German hometown ethos, sung at the point where the demise of the hometowns was irreversible, is Richard Wagner's *Die Meistersinger von Nürnberg* of 1868.[12] In 1871 Germany adopted the European norm and became, under Prussian rule, a unified nation-state. And it did so as the bearer of a particular cultural legacy—one in which nostalgia for an earlier, more pacific world could envisage an urban community exempt from the abstraction and anonymity of the modern industrial city.

What are the consequences of this legacy for the tradition of German prose that generates a novel such as *Buddenbrooks*? One crucial point emerges from our excursus into German social history. The European norm implies, as many commentators have stressed, a radical collision between public and private experience; the public realm is dominated by the competitive forces of the self-regulating market, whereas the private realm of family and home harbors the emotional needs of the self—compassion, gentleness, love. Yet, by contrast, both the reality and the myth of the "hometown" in the German lands did not generate such a sharp disjunction between the individual's private and public persona. The public realm was not an offense to the emotional needs of the individual, and the private realm, in its turn, bore the imprint of the institutional world beyond the confines of the home. I do not wish to impute to the German lands some kind of paradisal condition from which conflicts are banished once and for all. German prose is full of the frictions between public and private imperatives such as we find in the literature of European realism. But the interplay of public and private is conceptualized differently in German prose.

2

Buddenbrooks
and European Realism

Buddenbrooks is of quite particular interest within the German literary and cultural tradition, but its importance goes much further than that, for it brings into focus a number of crucial issues in regard to the European novel in general. *Buddenbrooks* is not only a supreme example of literary realism, but it is also a wonderfully intelligent reflection on the modes and allegiances of literary realism. It is a novel profoundly and richly about history, yet it also perceives the historicity of its own mode as symptomatic of one kind of novel, one kind of narrative history.

To understand the tradition from which *Buddenbrooks* was generated, it is important to consider a number of theoretical matters related to the theory and practice of European realism. Much recent critical theory, namely poststructuralism and deconstruction, has mounted a fearsome onslaught on many cherished assumptions of literary realism. The argument runs roughly as follows.[1]

1) It is false to assume that there is a literary text, on the one hand, and an extraliterary thing called reality, on the other, to which that text refers. What human beings apprehend as the reality around them is not simply unmediated facts and objects; it is, rather, a world

rendered habitable (i.e., intelligible) by a vast economy of signs, symbols, conventions, rituals, assumptions. The literary text is therefore but one text within the corporate textuality of a society.

2) Literature is constituted by language; it cannot, therefore, produce a semblance of the world but only a semblance of true discourse about the world.

3) Much theory of mimesis has, without realizing as much, conflated two categories of representational truthfulness: *vraisemblance* (that is, what looks truthful, coherent, and logical as an account of the world) and *bienséance* (that is, what is felt to be seemly or socially acceptable). Hence, the traditional work of novel realism—the convincing story of the way we live now, or lived then—does not in any genuine sense acquaint us with an experiential world outside its own functioning as a literary text. Rather, such a novel, insofar as it functions as the classic "readable" text, confirms us, our ideology, our discourse, our assumptions of what is relevant or irrelevant, central or peripheral. In so doing, it confirms tacit assumptions, making them seem ever more necessary, inalienably right, in a word, natural.

4) The philosophical naïveté of realism, to which I have already referred, is its most damaging property. Even the novel that looks as though it is critical of society merely suggests that there are certain things to be regretted, or questioned; but it leaves the essential worldview intact. What looks like criticism is mere tinkering that serves to confirm the prevailing assumptions with every line of the text.

I have summarized the "antirealistic" implications of modern critical theory not to be modish but because it seems to me that they raise genuinely important questions. The insistence on the textuality of the text can, at the very least, be welcomed as a corrective to the hasty politicization, to that rage for unmediated referentiality which characterized much literary scholarship in the 1970s. Moreover, we must surely take seriously the obvious—but for that reason often overlooked—fact that literature, even realistic literature, is made not of objects *(res)* but of language. For example, where a work of narrative fiction describes an armchair in a character's room, it gives us, by definition, words, signifiers, not the signified. The only way in which it could offer the latter is by enclosing an armchair with every copy of the text. The armchair is made of wood, horsehair, and upholstery, whereas the text is made, irreducibly, of words. But where a literary text invokes, as part of the story it has to tell, the assumptions, the values, the symbols, the clichés that are in social circulation, there is an overlap of medium between the literary text and the sociopsychological processes it chronicles. The values, thoughts, and assumptions of the characters' lives are all couched in language, as is the worded text that records them.

The overlap of medium gives us common ground with the characters. When we, the readers, perceive a situation, a scene, an object as something invested with symbolic value, we are engaged in a process to which the characters are also party. They, like us, symbolize events and experiences, they invest them with meaning. As readers, we are both implicated in these processes and superior to them. We have a measure of privileged overview in that we see the characters functioning within a model of human experiences that is relatively compact (and this remains true even of a long and digressive novel). The model, in other words, has edges. We see the human behavior charted in the text as *a* functioning world, and not as *the* world. We see the assumptions and values of a particular social world—the principles it holds to be self-evident and natural—not as "givens" but as "mades," not as existentially unalterable entities but as the products of the corporate, institutionalized subjectivity of a particular historical age.

What I am suggesting here is the possibility of a kind of prose fiction that may not be realistic in the traditional sense (i.e., concerning itself in large measure with things, with objects, with houses and streets and institutions) but that can nevertheless offer a profound comprehension of the extent to which individual life is caught up in the corporate mechanisms of a given society. I have in mind a narrative work that comprehends the society less in terms of physical evidence than at the level of shared values, ideas, and assumptions. Such a fiction would not be philosophically naive in the way that most European realism is. It would, rather, both reflect and reflect on the consciousness of a given age to make us aware of how ideas, principles, and assumptions shape the characters' lives and show them to be living in a particular time and place. In the process we would be alerted to the manifold ways in which social life is constituted—not only by the armchairs the characters can or cannot afford, but also by shared values and concepts, by certain agreements and conventions.

If the classics of the European novel provide superb examples of a realism of fact, setting, and outward event, we should not close our eyes to the possibility of a realism of concept and idea, of mental life. This latter possibility is exemplified most richly by the tradition of German narrative prose from the late eighteenth century onward—and it is from this tradition that *Buddenbrooks* was generated. We have done a great disservice to this tradition by seeing it as yet another example of the besetting German sin of inwardness. Generations of critics have assumed that where German fiction concerns itself with the mental life of its characters it seeks thereby to chart some timeless realm of abstract, free-floating ideas, a pantheon that is exempt from the pressures and concerns of social life. This interpretation does less than justice to a major narrative tradition because it converts novels and stories into mere pretexts for discursive philosophizing, whereas, time and time again, German fiction shows us that the inwardness it explores so richly is part of the narratively comprehended—that is, historicized—signature of a particular social world. As I suggested in my remarks on Mack Walker's study of the "hometowns," we are made to see that the subjectivity, the mental life, of the individual can bear the imprint of corporate (that is, social) concerns, and, that conversely, the public realm functions thanks to a consensus of values and assumptions that are anchored in the individual mind. The reflectiveness of the German novel invites us to attend to the symbols and concepts informing the characters' lives, but we are never allowed to forget that the occasion for these symbols and concepts is a narrative one, is a story, peopled by characters. This, as we shall see, is preeminently the case with *Buddenbrooks*.

Let me conclude this theoretical discussion with a brief historical footnote. It is worth remembering that the rise of the realistic novel is coterminal with the rise of the reflective, self-conscious novel. Henry

Fielding and Tobias Smollett are contemporaries of Laurence Sterne. The modern novel emerges as part of a complex process in which bourgeois self-confidence would seem to go hand in hand with bourgeois self-consciousness. Most critics would argue that the realistic novel and the self-conscious novel are mutually exclusive, and I certainly have no wish to claim that Sterne's *Tristram Shandy* is a realistic novel. But at the very least I would suggest that the simultaneity of the emergence of the two types of novel (and it may be, to take an earlier example, that in *Don Quixote* the overlap occurs in one and the same text) obliges us to modify the belief that once a novelist makes time and narrative room for thoughts and concepts, for an appeal to the reader's capacity for reflection, he thereby beckons us into some timeless (and therefore unrealistic) realm of pure discursive speculation.

Buddenbrooks is a supreme example of how novelistic strategies of inwardness, thoughtfulness, and reflectiveness can coexist with a realistic allegiance to the social and institutional substantiality of a specific historical world. It is a novel that fuses inwardness and outwardness; it makes the inner expressive of realistic concerns, and it makes realistic concerns not just outwardly accurate but also inwardly truthful insofar as they are shown to be inseparable from the abundantly portrayed psychological and mental life of the characters. Mann recognizes that even the forms of renegade inwardness, even the inner gestures of repudiating the values, assumptions, and expectations of the practical outer world, are imprinted by—and hence symptomatic of—that corporate culture. Yet the novel also accords to that inner life a measure of dignity, a certain cognitive value that inheres in the need to transcend the everyday and the practicable.

3

Critical Reception

With the appearance of the one-volume edition of *Buddenbrooks* in 1903, Thomas Mann's first novel became a best-seller, and it has retained the affection and respect of scholars and lay readers alike ever since—to say nothing of television and film audiences. Given the extraordinary success of the novel, any attempt at a full documentation of its critical reception becomes an overwhelming and, in the last resort, wearisome task.[1]

Of the initial responses to *Buddenbrooks*—and I am speaking here of those responses in which critical engagement with the text is serious—two instantly identifiable camps emerge. And these camps are still, *mutatis mutandis,* identifiable in recent criticism of the novel.

The first camp is based in Lübeck. The novel, once it hit home (literally and metaphorically), stirred up a hornet's nest. Thomas Mann, as we know, was perfectly prepared to draw extensively on the physical, psychological, and behavioral details of his own family and of his birthplace, Lübeck, and its inhabitants. Once Lübeck took note of the novel, there was outrage; many readers were convinced that the novel was a roman à clef, that its author had simply applied a thin veneer of fiction to disguise real people, and that, if one were in the know, one could establish not only who the real-life originals of the book's characters were but also what the novel was trying to say. The production of "keys" to the novel became a minor industry. Thomas Mann never denied that he had, indeed, borrowed extensively from authentic material in order to get the physical details right. But he was genuinely bemused that anybody could think that the hunt for the real-life basis of the work could be anything more than a parlor game. This bewilderment he expressed with unconcealed asperity in his essay "Bilse and I," where he argues that like a great many writers he may have used bits and pieces from his own autobiographical experience; but the result of that borrowing was one of transformation, was a process whereby facts, actualities, particularities were changed into the currency of fiction, into a realm of make-believe whose value or lack of it, whose importance or triviality, was to be judged by criteria not of testable accuracy but rather of felt truthfulness.

The Lübeck response to *Buddenbrooks* might well be left as an intriguing (or unedifying) footnote to literary history. If I mention it, it is because, at however unsubtle a level, it does, in fact, represent one whole strand in the reception of Mann's novel, that strand which perceives *Buddenbrooks* as a text that is vitally and significantly *about* the extraliterary and historically verifiable world of nineteenth-century German society. To my knowledge, the "who is who in Lübeck and *Buddenbrooks*" school of criticism has not prolonged its activities much beyond the first decade of the twentieth century. But in more thoughtful and sophisticated (though not unrelated) ways, Inge Diersen, Georg Lukács, and Hans Mayer,[2] among others, have sought to show that *Buddenbrooks* provides a genuine and important illumination of that extratextual world whose existence has been verified by the work of political scientists, sociologists, and historians.

The opposing camp is the one that responds to *Buddenbrooks* not in terms of its referentiality, not in terms of what it says about experiential realms outside its own aesthetic existence; rather, it sees the book essentially and primarily as a supreme example of sustained artistic craftsmanship. To take examples from the ranks of early critics, what Otto Grautoff, Kurt Martens, and Richard von Schaukal discern and esteem in *Buddenbrooks* is an astonishing piece of formal and structural organization.[3] Their voices express a perception of the novel that has continued to engage the critical community ever since. Put in simplified terms, we could say that, in contrast to those who assert that Mann's novel is "about society" or "about life," there is a whole chorus that perceives it as being "about itself." Critics of this persuasion draw attention to the fact that it is intensely structured, richly—almost claustrophobically—patterned, sustained by a dense web of leitmotivs, of parallel and contrasting scenes, of almost hermetic recurrences. Of late, this kind of argument has been advanced by such critics as Manfred Jurgensen, Helmut Koopmann, Herbert Lehnert, Peter Pütz, and Klaus-Jürgen Rothenberg.[4]

In a sense, it is always tempting for the most recent critic to lord it over his or her predecessors, to review the previous secondary literature with the sense of occupying a superior vantage point. Two observations are pertinent here. First, if (and it may be a very big "if") we are now in a superior position, it is because we can build, critically, on the work of our predecessors. They have given us our superiority; much of what we now take for granted we owe to them. Second, we may now—thanks to the work of our predecessors—be in a position to recognize that both camps of *Buddenbrooks* critics are, in a sense, right. It is an amazingly structured novel, so structured, indeed, that it never even begins to feel like a naive transcription of physical facts and events (which is often the kind of impression that traditional realistic novels give). But *Buddenbrooks* is also profound in its implications for our understanding of certain shifts in the values of nineteenth-century European society, and these implications are expressed through the density of artistic patterning that sustains the novel. It is because of—not in spite of—the novel's formal control that it speaks so richly and perceptively of extraliterary things.

I wish to suggest, then, that the antagonistic either/or approach characteristic of the two strands of critical reception is misleading. There is, I suspect, one particular theoretical issue that accounts for the critical impasse, and I shall examine it at the beginning of chapter 4. But I want to preface that discussion here by quoting from Hermann

Kurzke's recent study, *Thomas Mann, Epoche, Werk, Wirkung.* Kurzke is able to summarize the critical voices on Thomas Mann without ever becoming submerged in the clamor of disputing claims. No one who works on Mann can feel anything less than a sense of gratitude for what Kurzke accomplishes in his splendid volume. But precisely because Kurzke is so scrupulous, thoughtful, and perceptive in his own responses, the moments when he loses focus are the more striking—and, perhaps, they are indicative of where scholarship on Thomas Mann may have blurred rather than sharpened our responses as readers. Kurzke writes of *Buddenbrooks,*

> Thomas Mann is describing not a general, but rather a quite specific, development. The Buddenbrooks are not a typical nineteenth-century, middle-class family. Not even as an autobiography is the novel realistic. The Mann family did, admittedly, provide a whole number of individual features, but essentially it developed quite differently from the Buddenbrook family. Even the autobiographical elements are transposed into structural elements within a work of art. In this sense, the whole novel is a linguistic artifact based on specific philosophical theorems.[5]

With this judgment I disagree, and in the chapters that follow I shall endeavor to explain why.

A Reading

4

A "loose baggy monster"?

Much traditional theory of literary realism upholds as central the notion of redundant detail. The argument runs as follows. Realism, especially in the novel form, is abundantly about *res,* about palpable, outward experiences, about the practical world, about institutions, things, objects, and the ways in which they form (and deform) people's lives. This respect for sheer physical facts, for material "thereness," interlocks with the traditionally sanctioned untidiness of the novel genre; the extended epic form is allowed the luxury of leisureliness, spaciousness, indirection, of casual, unpurposeful attention to detail. I have in mind under this heading what Roland Barthes calls "the effect of the real" and what J. P. Stern has designated the realist's "emblems of plenty."[1] Common to both critics' perceptions is the notion that narrative realism must show itself to be creatively in love with things, facts, objects, with that simple and eloquent existence that has no need of further (aesthetic or human) justification. One does not have to look far for suitable examples: the opening of virtually any novel by Balzac or Dickens provides them.

I have no wish to deny the appeal of such narrative gestures that acknowledge the great plenitude of the physical universe. We recognize their rightness because we know that every fictional story that seeks to legitimize itself by re-creating for its setting an extrafictional physical world is, by definition, situated amidst a plurality of redundant things. Such acknowledgment of the redundant is, by one very potent convention, the very signature of realistic writing. I do wish, however, to question the notion that realistic novels have to be and feel like what Henry James has called "loose baggy monsters":

> A picture without composition slights its most precious chance for beauty, and is moreover not composed at all unless the painter knows *how* that principle of health and safety, working as an absolutely premeditated art, has prevailed. There may in its absence be life, incontestably, as *The Newcomes* has life, as *Les Trois Mousquetaires*, as Tolstoi's *Peace and War*, have it; but what do such large loose baggy monsters, with their queer elements of the accidental and the arbitrary, artistically *mean?*[2]

All novels are made up of words, of discourse, of narrative codes. If realism is a property of certain novel fictions, then it can only be a property of narrative registers and not of extraliterary facticity.[3] The acknowledgment of superfluous things does not provide unmediated contact with physical entities; it is a code, a trick of the novelist's trade. And novels can be sustained by other codes without forfeiting their realistic aims (and by such realistic aims one understands the concern to view and portray men's and women's experience as vitally and manifestly shaped by their outward social existence). *Buddenbrooks* neither is nor feels like a "loose baggy monster." Its density of artistic, stylistic, and symbolic organization is directed not at some poetic transcendence of the observable social world but rather at the articulation and comprehension of that world through art.[4]

Buddenbrooks opens in October 1835 with the family celebrating, at one of its traditional Thursday gatherings, in the company of both immediate and more distant relatives and of business associates and civic colleagues, the Buddenbrooks' recent purchase of the house in the Mengstrasse. Thomas is nine, Tony eight, and Christian seven.

A *"loose baggy monster"*?

The family and firm are represented by three generations, and as we, the readers, discover the new house along with the guests who are being shown around, we form an impression of great solidity and unity. The house shelters both family and firm and enshrines in its physical presence the various interlocking and mutually confirming strands of the Buddenbrook ethos, one that unites civic position, mercantile success, and dynastic, familial continuity. There are, admittedly, disturbing undercurrents to this seemingly placid world; Jean, the father of Thomas, Tony, and Christian, has a brief discussion with his father about Gotthold, the black sheep of the family, who has flouted family decorum by marrying beneath himself (and the family). Gotthold has written, asking, in the name of Christian charity, for money. Father and son debate the matter; the son, Jean is inclined to accede to Gotthold's request, but old Johann, his father, has no scruples about declining it. Gotthold has put himself beyond the pale—and there is an end to the matter.

Such undercurrents of conflict only briefly ruffle the grandiosely representative spectacle of the Buddenbrook ethos in its full panoply. But the subtitle of the novel—"Decline of a Family"—has the effect of alerting us to the first signs of disturbance. Jean, we note, has an inner life, a capacity for thoughtfulness and scruple that his father does not possess. And that inner voice, that renegade dimension of inwardness, which may be religious, artistic, or psychological in its primary manifestation, will grow stronger as the Buddenbrook story unfolds. The more it enables successive generations of the family to think, to ponder, and to dream, the less it allows them to discover in their inner life any convictions that are supportive of the weighty legacy of "being a Buddenbrook." The awakening inner life goes hand in hand with a weakening of physical health and well-being. It is this process of decline that the novel chronicles; it is this process that provides the governing thematic argument of the novel. The details reported by the novel are constantly shown to be symptomatic of that decline of which the subtitle so uncompromisingly speaks.

In 1842 old Johann and his wife, Antoinette, die. Thomas enters the firm and continues his education as a businessman with a spell in

Amsterdam. Tony, in the course of a traditional family holiday at Travemünde, meets and falls in love with one Morten Schwarzkopf, the son of the local lighthouse keeper. Morten is a medical student of progressive views. But the Buddenbrooks have had enough experience of mésalliance with the "Gotthold affair." Pressure is brought to bear on Tony, and she finally knuckles under to the family ethos and marries one Bendix Grünlich, a businessman from Hamburg. The family blackmailing of Tony is monstrous, but we must note that it is ultimately effective not just because of the external sanctions that are threatened but because the Buddenbrook values and expectations are so firmly lodged inside Tony's mind and heart that she has little mental, emotional, or even linguistic capacity with which to frame a resistance to Buddenbrook wisdom. Moreover, by agreeing to do the accepted thing she makes herself even more completely a Buddenbrook. And yet—and I shall return to this point later—neither she nor the novel itself entirely forgets Morten. Throughout her life she repeats little sayings and phrases that derive from her affair with him.

Admittedly, Tony has none of the eroding thoughtfulness and imaginative potential that are present in her brothers Thomas and Christian. But then, as a woman, she is not credited with such things. Basically, she has only one role within that value scheme in which she so fervently believes;[5] she is supposed to make a decent marriage. Her marriage to Grünlich does not, in the long run, fulfill the Buddenbrook desiderata. Tony does, admittedly, produce a child, Erika, thereby fulfilling part of the family's expectations. But after some five years of marriage, Grünlich goes bankrupt, Tony's father refuses to help, and Tony accordingly returns with her daughter to the one family that truly sustains her—the Buddenbrooks.

This is not, however, the end of Tony's attempts to find marital happiness. In the mid-1850s she marries Alois Permaneder, an easygoing Bavarian, and goes to live in Munich. At roughly the same time Thomas marries Gerda Arnoldsen, the wealthy, exotic, artistically gifted daughter of the Amsterdam family with whom the Buddenbrooks have well-established business ties. Outwardly, Thomas's marriage is brilliant, and is thoroughly in accordance with the demands of the Buddenbrook dynasty. But the marriage both expresses and exacerbates the divided allegiances within him. With part of his being he unremittingly serves the values of the Buddenbrook family and firm. But with his inner self, which he only rarely and unwillingly acknowledges, Thomas is appalled by the mindlessness and brutality of the practical world and by the demands that it makes upon him. Gerda's artistic, and above all musical, gifts, her exotic aloofness from all that Buddenbrook existence entails correspond to some of the promptings of Thomas's renegade inner self. So too, in a different way, does his brother Christian's neurotic, self-obsessed preference for theater and a dubious social life over a solid day's work at the office. In his repudiation of Christian, Thomas seeks to keep at bay his own ravaging uncertainties, but they continue to take their toll of his health and well-being.

Tony is not happy in her marriage to Permaneder. She feels uprooted in Munich, bereft of that confirmation of her identity which can come only from living in a society that shares her sense of the Buddenbrook ethos. Her estrangement from Permaneder is complete when one evening she catches him somewhat drunk and attempting to embrace a servant girl. Once again, she returns to the Buddenbrook home. Her attempt to contribute to the well-being and good standing of the family by means of her daughter Erika's marriage to one Hugo Weinschenk, who works for an insurance company, comes to nothing when Weinschenk is sent to prison for sharp practice. Daughter Erika, like her mother, returns to the family.

The decade of the 1860s is not without its brilliant successes: Thomas is elected a senator, he has a magnificent new house built in the Fischergrube, the firm celebrates its centenary in 1868. Even so, the signs of strain begin to show. Through a mixture of indecision, incaution, and bad luck, Thomas loses money, and with the death of his mother Elisabeth, the presiding spirit and supreme agent of family cohesion disappears from the scene. Thomas and Gerda have only one child, called Johann after his grandfather and great-grandfather but known as Hanno. He is a sickly, musically gifted boy—the "sensitive latecomer" of Mann's original project—who has no relationship at all to the practical obligations of being head of the family and firm that await him. His father dies of a stroke in 1875, and Hanno dies of typhoid in 1877. The process at the heart of Mann's novel thereby comes to its appointed end.

Tony Buddenbrook is present in both the opening and the closing scenes of the novel, and the contrast is cruel. Where the opening scene shows her embedded in three generations of the family, the final scene depicts her surrounded by a group of women. Gerda is about to return to Amsterdam to live with her father, leaving Tony with her daughter and with the relatives and hangers-on who constitute what is left of the family. Tony has none of the physical weakness and psychological rootlessness of the later male Buddenbrooks, but even she partakes of the decline that afflicts the Buddenbrooks—and she does so, paradoxically, because she tries so hard to place her life in the service of the Buddenbrook ethos. Tony fails, but certainly not for want of trying. Her nephew Hanno never even tries. Either way, the fatal engine of decline would seem to work ineluctably, and it makes its presence felt everywhere in the novel—in details of physical appearance and behavior, in the psychology of the characters, in the recurrent rhythms of family life (the festivals, the births and deaths, the holidays), in the details of the Buddenbrooks' economic life, in their artistic, and above all musical, leanings. Indeed, we might say that everything in this novel is, or at any rate seems to be, symptomatic, symptomatic of an overall thematic and stylistic design whereby each detail, each repeated phrase and leitmotiv conspires to articulate the decline of the family. It is this almost claustrophobic sense of a totally patterned novel about heavily patterned lives that makes *Buddenbrooks* the very antithesis of a "loose baggy monster."

The central and unavoidable question *Buddenbrooks* poses, then, is: What are we to make of this process of decline? Is it essentially a psychological process or biological or socioeconomic—or is it a philosophical one in that the novel adheres to a schematic design that declares inwardness the enemy of outwardness and says that thought, reflectiveness, and scruple can only be bought at the price of paralysis in the sphere of practical living? Certain critics[6] have, indeed, argued that the novel essentially conforms to a philosophical blueprint. I believe that we must resist the temptation to ascribe the process of decline to any one primary cause or motivation. With respect to the causality behind the events prescribed, *Buddenbrooks* hedges its bets; ultimately, it seeks to persuade us that social, economic, psychological, artistic, and philosophical considerations all contribute to the sequence of events it recounts. There is, in other words, no one cause of the Buddenbrook decline.[7]

Realistic novels, it is often said, reflect a certain social world. Such notions have been advanced not only by critics and theoreticians but also by novelists themselves. In the second chapter of *Our Mutual Friend* Dickens links descriptive narrative to the images in the "great looking-glass above the sideboard"; in the epigraph to chapter 13 of *The Red and the Black* Stendhal likens the novel to a "mirror passing along a road." Yet in spite of the currency granted to notions of mirroring, we would do well to remember that realism is not only a reflection *of* but also a reflection *on* the social world it portrays and interprets. *Buddenbrooks* is concerned to convey not just outwardly observable behavior but also inner life—imaginative, psychological, or philosophical. As successive generations of Buddenbrooks come to think, they find themselves questioning the legacy they have inherited. If the novel becomes, then, more reflective and inward as it unfolds, it does so because its theme demands it. The mode of the novel interlocks with the mode of being of the characters themselves. The narrative partakes of the characters' reflectiveness. The patterns they enact in their lives become more and more the object of their scrutiny and criticism, and the symbols by which they are required to live are examined and found wanting. These symbols are intimately related to the observable texture of the characters' lives; they are as much a part of their way of life as the chairs and sofas on which they sit. The Buddenbrooks are what they are by virtue of that physical and mental furniture that defines and articulates their lives. And the novel is faithful to both kinds of furniture, reflecting them and reflecting on them.

Balzac's *Père Goriot* opens with some 40 pages describing a seedy boardinghouse in Paris and delights in the sheer physical "thereness" of the details of the empirical world. The opening of *Buddenbrooks*—also 40 pages, concerning itself with one evening in October 1835—likewise introduces us to a palpable, physical world, one that has, in Henry James's phrase, "solidity of specification."[8] In *Buddenbrooks,* however, none of this solidity is described for its own sake; this is not narrative largesse or splendid redundancy. Mann's exposition is, in hindsight, overwhelming in its targeted relevance[9] in a way that is not true of *Père Goriot.*

5

Family Occasions

Buddenbrooks begins by plunging us *in medias res,* with a question posed by eight-year-old Tony and picked up by her grandfather. The question is, as we realize almost immediately, not a genuine request for information; it is a quotation rather than an actual question. Tony has been reciting her catechism and gets briefly stuck; her mother prompts her, whereupon she is able to resume her recitation without difficulty. The opening register of the novel has, then, essentially to do with ritual, with ritual statements being rehearsed.

After a mere two pages the details of the whole scene before us come wonderfully into focus. The characters are named in their family relationship to each other; we discover who and where the grandfather and mother-in-law are. We also discover, and are invited to share in the omnipresence of, dynastic family thinking. The grandmother, Madame Antoinette Buddenbrook, is, we learn, "née Duchamps." Her daughter-in-law Elisabeth, who is sitting next to her on the sofa, was, we learn, a Kröger before her marriage, and she has retained the characteristic laugh of the Krögers.

Initially, then, we register above all family roles, identities, and continuities. We are manifestly in a world in which identity is inseparable from lineage and continuity. This principle holds true also for the larger social and civic order; Tony's parents are referred to not only by their Christian names (Jean and Elisabeth) but also as "Konsul" and "Konsulin." No explanation is offered for these unusual titles. It is almost as though the narrator takes it for granted that we, the readers, are in the know and therefore do not have to be told (just as the narrator seems to assume that we know who the Krögers are and that they have a characteristic way of laughing). The narrative stance exudes the self-evidentness of a totally established way of life. As the story unfolds, certain details will become clear. We will discover, for example, that the head of the Buddenbrook family and firm is a key figure in trade both within the German lands and with other countries; and in consequence, as a mark of respect and trust, that senior Buddenbrook acquires a diplomatic role and the title "Konsul" to go with it.

The exposition never allows us to forget that civic identity which is so much a part of the characters before us. The catechism from which Tony is reciting has, we learn, been reissued in 1835 in a revised form, "with the approval of a high and most wise Senate" (I, 1, 3). Again, the narrator takes information for granted; we are not told *which* senate, just as we are not told in which town we find ourselves. We are, however, left in no doubt that the town, with its civic administration (the Senate and other offices), exists and that it is fully operative in the lives that concern us. The characters whom we are gradually learning to identify have a familial and civic role, and, as the exposition unfolds, we will also learn of the economic and mercantile roles that fall to the men as breadwinners. Everything interlocks to suggest the solidity of a way of life that is held together by multiple networks of value and significance. Continuity is to be sensed everywhere. We learn that this gathering is taking place on a Thursday, and on this day, every fortnight, the family comes together. The German reads: "Es war Donnerstag, der Tag an dem ordnungsmässig jede zweite Woche die Familie zusammenkam." The adverb *ordnungsmässig* implies both "by tradition" and "in accordance with statutes and orders." The notion, then, of sustaining ritual, or ordered and orderly lives, is as much a part of Tony's reciting the catechism as it is of everything else that occurs during these regular Thursday gatherings.

This principle of regulated family life, which is first enunciated in the masterly exposition, provides the underlying rhythm for the plot of Mann's novel. Time and time again we witness family occasions of one kind or another. Many years later, for example, Hanno, like Tony before him, will grind to a halt while trying to recite a text he has learned by heart. But in Hanno's case, the text is a poem; and, unlike Tony, he cannot pick up the thread and complete his recitation. The scene ends with Hanno's tears and Thomas's anger. We will recall the opening scene of the novel, and we will do so with a sense of the changes in sensibility and character that make the later gathering more problematic and gloomy than the opening one.

Toward the end of part I, Jean's eyes alight on one of two mottoes that accompany the Buddenbrooks throughout the novel. This one is emblazoned over the front door of the Mengstrasse house: *Dominus providebit* (The Lord will provide). The other motto is the injunction, passed from father to son, to make good business by day but only such business as allows for a good night's sleep afterwards. This motto derives very precisely from the one to be found in the papers of Thomas Mann's own family: "My son, work readily by day, but make only such business that we may sleep peacefully at night."[1] The interplay of business acumen and Christian scruple raises many key issues in regard to the novel's social import, to which I will return later. Here I wish to concentrate on two notions introduced in the exposition that recur throughout the novel. One is that of the family chronicle. The motto about sleeping easily at night is enshrined in the family chronicle, which is the history of the various generations as recorded by each family head. The point of the chronicle—and in the mid-nineteenth century the great German social historian W. H. Riehl wrote about its importance for the integrity of house and family—was that it was precisely not a private diary[2]; it recorded not thoughts, intuitions, moods, but the key events of family life and above all else the values transmitted through successive generations. In this sense, the motto is inalienably part both of the chronicle that expresses continuity in and for the family and of Mann's chronicling novel itself.

The other notion, common to both the mottoes we are considering, is that of inwardness, specifically of religious belief. In part I we register the first intimations of the process of decline that runs through the novel. It is, as we have already seen, a decline that is very much bound up with the emerging inner life. Jean, as part I shows us in the discussion concerning Gotthold, is more prone to religious fervor and religious scruple than is his father. The process the novel charts begins, then, in part I, and is inseparably bound up with the attempt of successive Buddenbrook generations to sustain an increasingly unworkable continuity. From this is generated the characteristic rhythm of the novel: events recur, familial occasions repeat themselves. And as they do so, we notice both sameness and difference, both outward continuity and the inner disarray wrought by processes of ineluctable decline, by inward changes that ultimately impinge on the outward solidity of the Buddenbrooks.

Of course, many of the changes in individual family members are highlighted precisely by their attempt not to change. By tradition, the Buddenbrook family holiday is taken by the sea, at Travemünde. There are three extended descriptions of a visit by a Buddenbrook to the resort: Tony's stay when she meets Morten (part III, chapters 5–13), Hanno's last blissful holiday (part X, chapter 3), and Thomas's more brief and gloomy visit (part X, chapter 6). All three of them rejoice to escape from their everyday existence; they delight in the sea; they all register some sense of deprivation when they have to leave Travemünde and return home. But for Tony, the return, although it is overshadowed by the family's pressure on her to marry Grünlich, is a reentry into what she feels to be an essentially benign and supportive world. Neither Thomas nor Hanno share that perception. Both sense the ominous embrace of an alien and brutal way of life. Both—Hanno even more radically than his father—feel the beauty of the sea as an almost metaphysical force. The sea is all unindividuated flux and energy, a primal substance beyond the parameters of normal human knowing and feeling. When Thomas and Hanno experience the sea, they do more than simply get away from the stresses and strains of everyday obligations; they touch a profound truth that challenges all notions of social and practical achievement.

Inevitably, one of the family events that recurs is the death of one or another of its members. Each time this happens, rituals are observed whose aim is to cocoon the family from the stark brutality and finality of death through expressions of decorum and reassuring tradition. The early Buddenbrooks are not prepared for death: old Johann and his wife Antoinette are almost surprised that mortality, as it were, applies to them. When they discover their energies waning and in consequence have to confront a situation in which they can no longer take part in the familiar rituals and customs of being Buddenbrooks, they find themselves willy-nilly plucked out of their reassuring routine and invited to reflect on it, to question it and themselves. And all such un-Buddenbrook-like experiences are incomprehensible to them. To move to the other end of the spectrum (and the novel), Hanno's death from typhoid is the culmination of a long and intense death wish, which is expressed with sexual abandon in his music. He has no second thoughts about leaving behind him the real world of Buddenbrook existence.

In between the deaths of old Johann and his wife and of Hanno we have Jean's rapid death as oppressive heat gives way to cooling cloudburst, and Elisabeth's bitter, resentful battle with death as she fights every inch of the way to retain her hold on the world that has hitherto sustained her completely. When finally, weakened by the appalling pain and struggle, she does let go, it is in the name of being reunited with the dead Buddenbrooks beyond the grave. For Elisabeth, it seems, continuity is all. And there is Thomas's death—swift, undignified, and brutal; the anguished brain spins ever more tightly in upon itself to the point where it explodes into extinction. Such moments all bear the characteristic imprint of *Buddenbrooks* in that they are points of precisely explored change within continuity. The narrative framework for this all-important perception of familial decline is superbly initiated in the exposition.

So minutely organized is *Buddenbrooks* as a text that even tiny textual details enshrine the central design of continuity and change. Part I provides illustrations of what I have in mind, for even small, low-key incidents and modest, unemphatic formulations contribute to the novel's density of statement. We have already registered the fact that Jean, in his religious feeling, betrays an inwardness that is alien to his father. The old man, we note, is not above teasing Tony about her catechism, relishing the fact that she cannot understand whole tracts of what she is reciting. Later, at the beginning of chapter 10, he will tease his son about being "on intimate terms with the Almighty" (I, 10, 32). But when they begin to discuss the matter of Gotthold's request for money, weighty differences in temperament and attitude come to the fore, and a number of subtle hints make it clear that what is being enacted here is a significant change from one generation to the next. Jean is defenseless before Gotthold's appeal to Christian charity. But old Johann has no difficulty in crushing that offense to commercial good sense:

> Unchristian feelings! Ha! Very tasteful, I must say,—this pious crav-
> ing for money! What sort of a bunch are you young people, eh?
> Your heads full of Christian and fanciful idiocies ... and ...
> idealism! And we old folks are the heartless mocking spirits ... and
> you with the July monarchy and your practical ideals. (I, 10, 35)

Much later in the novel, the narrator takes over the implicit gen-
eralization in the old man's words when he comments on that vulnerability which is characteristic of the son's generation—Jean has begun
to weaken when Grünlich, in despair at his bankruptcy, threatens sui-
cide if his father-in-law declines to help him:

> Johann Buddenbrook leaned back in his armchair, pale, his heart
> pounding. For the second time this man's feelings, whose expression
> bore the imprint of complete honesty, laid siege to him, ... once
> again the effusive reverence of his generation for human feelings
> went right through him—which had always run counter to his dis-
> passionate and practical business sense. (IV, 8, 176)

In this passage the narrator refers us to an earlier meeting between Jean and Grünlich. But the echoes run farther back than that—to the exposition of the novel, to Gotthold's appeal for charity. What is at stake throughout these scenes is a perception of change at work both within the Buddenbrook family and in society at large. The Buddenbrook psyche is symptomatic of a changing cultural temper.

Part I of the novel, then, illuminates a number of significant differences between Jean and his father. The following passage of dialogue is characteristic, and its implications extend throughout the novel. Jean is talking about the Ratenkamps, who built the splendid house in the Mengstrasse that the Buddenbrooks have just acquired. The Ratenkamps were, it seems, a successful family and firm who recently went into irretrievable decline. Disaster was complete when the last head of the family and firm, Dietrich Ratenkamp, took on a totally unreliable and largely impoverished man named Geelmaack as his partner. Jean gloomily reflects that Dietrich was thereby acquiescing in, and accelerating, the inevitable:

> "But I believe that Dietrich Ratenkamp necessarily and unavoidably had to link up with Geelmaack in order that destiny might take its course. . . . He must have acted under the pressure of an inexorable necessity. . . . He was paralyzed."
>
> "*Assez,* Jean," said old Buddenbrook, putting his spoon to one side. "That is another one of your *idées.*" (I, 4, 15–16)

Old Johann, as we know from the opening pages of the novel, is fond of using French as well as the local dialect. He employs both registers for the emphatic dismissal of what he perceives as pretentious nonsense. *Assez* is one of his favorite words, bespeaking impatience with attitudes or behavior he finds silly. Here he dismisses his son's gloomy metaphysical speculation as yet another example of that undisciplined inner life which threatens to overturn practical common sense. More than 200 pages later, the narrator comments that Jean was the first of his line to know "unfamiliar, un-bourgeois, and differentiated feelings" (V, 2, 202f.). The sequence of the three adjectives is important;

that which is not of the everyday world is not of the bourgeois world; and Jean's feelings are "differentiated" in the sense that they do make distinctions of which the integrated bourgeois mind is largely unaware.

It is one of the great achievements of *Buddenbrooks* that it refrains from simple value judgments on the recurrent themes and issues with which it so richly confronts us. While it does enlist our sympathies for the increasingly problematic Buddenbrooks, it never allows us to forget the virtues of the older generation. This generosity of understanding and sympathy is part of the glory of the novel. One tiny but eloquent illustration of this, again from the exposition, has to do with views of education. In the passage already quoted in which old Johann reproaches Jean with weakness in the matter of Gotthold's request for money, he refers sarcastically to the idealism of the younger generation and mentions (somewhat cryptically) the "July monarchy and your practical ideals" (I, 10, 35). The reference is to an earlier discussion at the dinner table in which Jean makes clear his sympathies for the progressive spirit of Louis-Philippe and the July monarchy and for the "practical ideals" they seek to serve. Old Johann disagrees in the following terms:

> "Practical ideals . . . naw, I'm not for 'em." In his irritation he fell into dialect. "Everywhere business academies and technical academies and commercial schools are springing up overnight, and the grammar school and classical education are stupid, a *bêtise*, and the whole world thinks of nothing but mines and industry and money-making." (I, 5, 20)

A mere 35 pages from the end of the novel, we will have occasion to recall the old man's words. In a chapter of unforgettable power we are given a description of the anguish that Hanno Buddenbrook undergoes during a typical school day. The narrator comments on the aggressive, brutal spirit that characterizes the new regime of the school: "Where once upon a time classical education had been respected as an aim in itself that one pursued at a gentle and leisurely pace and with cheerful idealism, now the terms authority, duty, power, service, career were installed as the highest virtues" (XI, 2, 565). The reference to the classics and to idealism is enough to make the link back to that early scene in part I, to make us reflect that the older world may have had, in certain fields at any rate, more humanity and generosity of spirit than the modern world knows.

It is a measure of the superlative artistic control of *Buddenbrooks* that so many of the themes and motifs that sustain the novel are initiated in part I, in that leisurely sequence of 10 chapters devoted to a family occasion which eavesdrops on largely casual conversation and forms an exposition that feels anything but momentous or portentous. The novel's opening is both intensely significant and utterly unemphatic. One is reminded of Mann's tribute to his countryman Theodor Fontane, a novelist supremely adept in his handling of narrative conversation: "People often called him a 'conversationalist,' and he himself did so. But the truth is that he was a singer."[3] In his exposition to *Buddenbrooks* Mann manages something similar. He eavesdrops with apparently disarming casualness while at the same time introducing what will be key organizational motifs in the novel.

The brief exchange in which old Johann and Jean disagree good-humoredly about the Buddenbrooks' garden behind the Burgtor is a prime example of how subtly Mann infuses dialogue with implication. The old man would love to have it tidied up, the grass cut, the trees trimmed; Jean, on the other hand, resists and praises the delights of the garden as untrammeled nature. The difference of opinion is a significant difference in cultural sensibility between eighteenth-century mentality and that of the nineteenth. The old man, whose manner of dress marks him out as somebody formed by the previous century, likes the formal garden, whereas his son delights in untamed nature and thereby speaks in favor of the so-called English garden that became popular in Europe in the later eighteenth and early nineteenth century as romanticism took hold. The English garden was frequently just as much the result of deliberate landscaping as was the formal, or French, garden. But the results were quite different. The English garden was asymmetrical; it was meant to look natural, artless. The formal garden was nature regimented by the hand of man. Behind a few lines of simple conversation we sense the broader currents and patterns of sociocultural change.[4] The decline that transforms the Buddenbrook family as the novel unfolds partakes, as we shall see, of a larger process of historical change.

6

Psychology and Character Drawing

The portrayal of the characters in *Buddenbrooks,* both of their outward appearance and of their inner state, is noteworthy for its economy and expressiveness; once again Thomas Mann's skill shows itself in his ability to sustain narrative arguments that constantly mediate between the presence of continuity and the processes of change. With respect to character drawing too, part I initiates a number of registers that will recur throughout the novel. It is, for example, worth noticing the moment when Thomas and Christian join the family gathering direct from school. Their first entry in the novel is symptomatic of what is to come. Christian, on being asked about his day at school, mimics one of the teachers, to which his brother responds: "Thomas, who lacked such gifts, stood next to his younger brother and laughed heartily and without envy. His teeth were not particularly fine, but small and yellowish" (I, 2, 10). The physical detail of Thomas's appearance that is mentioned—the poor state of his teeth—becomes a refrain throughout the novel. Thomas's death will in part be brought about by a hideously painful tooth condition. And the weakness will emerge even more radically in Hanno whose teeth will cause him almost constant suffering. Hanno inherits his bad teeth from his father;

he also inherits the bluish shadows under the eyes that are so insepa-rable from his mother Gerda's exotic beauty. The crucial notion of continuity as physical, genetic transmission of observable features from one generation to the next receives its most ominous formulation at the end of part V. Thomas and Tony have been discussing Gerda's strange, artistic temperament. The door opens:

> The heavy, dark red hair framed the white face, and in the corners
> of the close-set brown eyes there lurked blueish shadows.
>   It was Gerda, mother of future Buddenbrooks. (V, 9, 236)

At one level, the final sentence in this passage must surely be taken as the narrator's ironic quotation of family expectations. At another, it serves to suggest the force of heredity: *Buddenbrooks* is a novel that belongs in part to the European naturalist movement with its concern to trace scientifically definable processes of causality and determinism. In the *Reflections of an Unpolitical Man*, Mann comments on the "completely European literary air that blows" in *Buddenbrooks*, and he goes on to claim that "it is for Germany perhaps the first and only naturalistic novel."[1] Heredity became, for obvious reasons, a key theme with the naturalist generation. Its presence can be noted in Mann's novel as the leitmotivs of physical description recur to express the processes—both physical and spiritual—that are ineluctably at work in the Buddenbrook heredity.

Thomas is acutely aware of the processes of physical decline that are at work in his own, and his son's, body. He consumes his energies in trying to resist the signs and symptoms of this decline, in trying to preserve the Buddenbrook line as one of physical intactness. But in so doing, he achieves at best histrionic success; he is able to look the part, but the gulf between outward appearance and the truth of his selfhood becomes ever more unbridgeable. As Thomas's plight becomes increas-ingly desperate, so the descriptions intensify of those ghastly moments of truth when he is alone and can let the efficient mask drop from his unspeakably weary face. The narrative prose becomes impassioned in its expression of the full extent of his suffering:

> Truly, Thomas Buddenbrook's existence was nothing more than
> that of an actor—but an actor whose whole life, right down to the
> smallest and most mundane detail, has become one single act of
> self-representation, one which—with the exception of a few rare
> and brief hours of solitariness and relaxation—constantly claimed
> and consumed all his forces. (X, 1, 480)

In part I, when the two brothers are first introduced to us, Christian, as we recall, mimics one of his teachers, and Thomas laughs
"without envy." That simple statement encapsulates and prefigures
much of the complex psychological relationship between Thomas and
Christian that subsequently develops. Thomas despises Christian for
his weakness and frivolity, for his incapacity and unwillingness even
to try to serve the Buddenbrook ethos. Yet it is because he understands
all too well the weakness in Christian that he refuses him all sympathy
and goodwill; in keeping Christian at bay, he is also keeping his own
weakness at bay. Something similar informs Thomas's attitude of
willed incomprehension toward his son Hanno; it is because he understands the boy all too well that Thomas will not allow himself to
show even a modicum of understanding toward his son. Such dramas
of acknowledgment and repudiation give psychological resonance to
two supreme moments of truth in the later sections of the novel. In
one, the smoldering resentment between Thomas and Christian comes
to a head in an appalling quarrel; in the other, a moment of all too
brief communion and sympathy between father and son comes into
being—and is then destroyed.

The occasion for the bitter quarrel between Thomas and Christian is initially the family council that meets to decide on the distri-
bution of the effects that had belonged to their mother. Christian is
unusually acquisitive, which surprises Thomas, who had assumed that
most of their mother's things would be of no interest to his brother. It
turns out that Christian is intending soon to marry one Aline Puvogel.
Thomas is appalled at what he sees as the outward and visible sign of
everything that is feckless and irresponsible about his brother. Christian resents Thomas's automatic assumption that he occupies the
moral high ground and accuses him of coldness and bigotry. The row,

like so many quarrels of this kind, is unedifying and embarrassing. Slights and injuries from the past are dredged up as insults are traded in a bitter battle fueled by years of pent-up resentment. (At one point Thomas and Christian each compete for the accolade of being more ill than the other!)

The scene is absolutely superb in its comprehension of psychological tensions[2] and of the multiple ways in which such corrosive feelings touch the very nerve centers of the persons involved, the values by which they endeavor to live. In the midst of the lacerating battle between the brothers moments of truth emerge that even the two combatants recognize. Christian says to Thomas, "You are so utterly devoid of compassion and love and humility. . . . Ah! . . . How sick I am of it all, the tact, the propriety, the emotional balance, the poise and dignity. . . . I am sick to death of it." The reproach to Thomas— that his self-control and decorum are indistinguishable from coldness of heart—is not without cogency. And Thomas recognizes this in a moment that combines both acknowledgment and repudiation of his brother: "I have become as I am . . . because I did not want to become like you. If I have inwardly shunned you, it was because I had to be on my guard against you, because your being and character are a threat to me. . . . I am speaking the truth" (IX, 2, 454). Here we get a sense of the almost internecine closeness of family life in the Buddenbrook model: each member of the family as it were carries the others around with him or her.

The second high point in terms of the novel's psychological argument comes when Thomas and Hanno meet in a moment of shared anguish. Thomas resents his literal and metaphorical exclusion from Gerda's music making. She regularly receives a Lieutenant von Trotha, and Thomas is resentful of the time they spend together. In an unguarded moment, he comes close to admitting the full extent of his wretchedness to Hanno:

> And behold, at these words little Johann opened his golden brown eyes wide and turned them with a large, and clear, and loving gaze as never before, to his father's face. . . . God knows how much he

understood. But one thing was certain, and both of them felt it—
that in these seconds, as their eyes met, every strangeness and coldness, every constraint and misunderstanding that had come between
them fell away; that Thomas Buddenbrook here and whenever energy, efficiency, and clear-eyed freshness were not required but
rather fear and suffering were at issue, could be sure of the trust
and devotion of his son. (X, 5, 507)

The intensity of the narrator's rhetorical assertion is unmistakable.
Passionately the narrative voice commends this moment to us as one
of truth, sympathy, and communion between two characters. They
meet at the level of a shared understanding that fear and suffering are
the inalienable truths of human life—not energy and success. What
Thomas and Hanno share is a revulsion at the sheer stress and brutality of the living process; their moment of communion is one in
which the inwardness and reflectiveness that are so much a part of the
Buddenbrook decline are actually shared, and potentially create a
communion of those who are not on the side of life. Here, once again,
the wonderfully sustained psychological strand intersects with the
philosophical strand of the novel's import.

As I have noted, the philosophical design implicit in *Buddenbrooks* rests on the notion of a distinct gulf between reflectiveness and
active living: those who come to analyze and question their experience
seem incapable of living their lives with any commitment and zest. In
any consideration of the psychological strand within the novel it is
important to note that the philosophical scheme that sunders *Geist*,
"mind," from *Leben*, "life," can also be expressed in more immediate
terms as a familiar aspect of everyday psychology. Put simply, it entails
the experience we have all had that once we become conscious of ourselves and our actions, we become clumsy and awkward where for-
merly we were skillful and relaxed. The term *self-conscious* in English
implies not only a philosophical notion (having to do with our being
aware of ourselves as living beings) but also (and more frequently) a
psychological one (of being embarrassed or awkward). It is in terms
of this double meaning that the philosophical and psychological arguments of *Buddenbrooks* run together so richly.

The first page of the novel gives us a lightweight and charming illustration of what is involved. Tony is reciting her catechism; almost without warning, she is aware of herself uttering a question—"What is that?"—and her automatic recitation suddenly comes to a standstill. Her mother prompts her, she picks up the thread, and rattles off the remainder of the article of the catechism like clockwork. Tony has just experienced the psychological truth to which I have just referred—that thinking may prevent doing. She formulates it to herself in the following terms: "When you were in the swing of it, she thought, it was just like going down the 'Jerusalem Mountain' in winter on the small sledge with your brothers: all thoughts went out of your head, and you could not stop even if you wanted to" (I, 1, 9). It is ironic that Tony's vision of splendidly inevitable physical movement is one of descent; the descent or decline of the Buddenbrooks occurs with much of the physical inevitability of a sledge accelerating down a snow-covered slope. As we shall see, one of the chief agents in that process will be precisely the thinking, knowing mind that saps the will to live.

7

Narrative Technique:
Temporal and Spatial Specifications

In two recent papers[1] Lilian Furst has reminded us that one of the most familiar and persuasive codes of literary realism is that which provides for specificity of temporal and spatial indicators. It is noteworthy how abundantly this code is represented in *Buddenbrooks*. The opening pages are, for example, replete with a sense of place: we are witnessing a particular kind of housewarming party, and we follow the visitors on their conducted tour through the new house. Indeed, time and time again we are placed by the narrative voice in a position of complicity—almost physical contiguity—with the family group. I have already drawn attention to the self-evidentness of the narrative gesture, of designating Elizabeth and Jean as "Konsulin" and "Konsul." Often the pronoun *man*, meaning "one," is used, and this manages to imply a collectivity of which the readers are part.[2] Because English uses this pronominal form much less easily and naturally than does German, the translations tend to sound very stilted:

> One was sitting in the "landscape room" on the first floor of the spacious old house in the Mengstrasse which the firm of Johann Buddenbrook had acquired some time ago. (I, 1, 5).

Through a glass door that was opposite the windows one could look into the half darkness of a hall flanked with pillars. (6)

For the sake of Madame Buddenbrook the Elder one had already installed the double windows. (6)

In these examples we become almost "one of the family," and it is important to spell out the implications of the pronoun *man*. The exposition of this novel is one in which readers are given much topographical information so that they may situate the story within precise temporal and spatial parameters. But equally, the exposition is never stilted in its conveying of information. Casualness prevails: often we find ourselves eavesdropping on snippets of conversation. Even passages of straightforward narratorial description are, if anything, allusive; as I have already suggested, rather than being overtly informative, they assume us to be in the know.[3] We do, of course, acquire a very precise sense of the geography of the house. But even this is done in the most understated way possible, and once again by drawing on the implicit *man* of the particular descriptive mode. We join the group that is being shown round the house. This characteristic narrative gesture means that the physicality of the world is taken for granted, just as it is taken for granted that the story takes place in Lübeck, although the name of the town is never, in fact, mentioned. The names of the streets and of other topographical features make it clear. The not naming of the town is part of the rhetorical device that assumes we already have our bearings in this world. To name the actual town would be supererogatory, like telling a Londoner who is reading a novel in which the hero buys a cup of coffee in Leicester Square that the novel is set in London (and not in Leicester).

This narrative gesture of imputed complicity, of assuming that we know where we are almost before we have begun reading the novel, is immensely potent. We have not been reading long before we—like the family put before us—take the world in which the novel is set for granted. Moreover, when reference is made, on the first page of the novel, to the catechism having been recently reedited under the aegis of a "high and truly wise Senate," we find ourselves, almost before we realize it, participating in the respect for the Senate. Of course we have no evidence to tell us that this body is wise; we simply take the family's (and the narrator's) word for it.

Similarly, certain tiny hints in the form of adverbial conjectures compound our sense of being not so much readers of a novel as participants in a real social event. For instance, when Tony's grandfather starts to tease her about the catechism she has just recited, we read: "He laughed with delight at being able to make fun of the catechism, and he had probably only initiated this little examination with such an end in view" (I, 1, 4). Then a few pages later, at the beginning of chapter 2, the arrival of the town's poet, Jean Jacques Hoffstede, is reported. We are told that he "undoubtedly had for today a few verses in his coat pocket" (I, 2, 9). We should note the force of the adverbs "probably" *(wahrscheinlich)* in the first quotation and "undoubtedly" *(sicherlich)* in the second. If we were literal-minded readers, we would no doubt immediately register the inconsistency inherent in such gestures of conjecture. We would presumably object that we are reading a novel, not a newspaper report of an actual event, and consequently we would have to insist that the narrator of the story must know whether or not old Johann made Tony recite her catechism in order that he might be able to air his somewhat skeptical views on religious matters. We might also say that the narrator must know whether Herr Hoffstede has some verses with him or not. But we do not, in fact, react in this way. We know that we are being asked to collude with one of those conventions whereby the narrative perspective of a fiction is made to heighten the sense of genuine (that is, nonliterary) reality. The convention entails the narrative voice's abstaining from its usual privileged access to the inner lives of the characters in order to adopt the persona of being one character among the other characters. The narrative voice in *Buddenbrooks* is by no means exclusively aligned with this perspective, however; elsewhere the narrative will betray a totally privileged intimacy with the private thoughts, intuitions, and impulses of the characters. But that register coexists with that of the narrator's being no more than one of the participants at the family occasion.

Buddenbrooks is replete with careful indications of time—specifically with respect to the years in which events occur. In part I, toward the end of chapter 6, we hear Hoffstede's poem (of course he had one with him!) in celebration of the new house. On many subsequent occasions the novel will remind us of this poem and the occasion it commemorates. The poem exists not only as something recited; Hoffstede has written it down, and the page has at the top a clear naming and dating of the occasion being celebrated: "On the occasion of friendly participation in the joyous celebration consecrating the newly acquired house with the Buddenbrook family. October 1835" (I, 6, 23). As the story of the Buddenbrooks unfolds, we will be enabled to date events with extraordinary precision. In this sense, we are again on a par with the family, because many of the moments of dating occur as quotations from the family chronicle, which is kept punctiliously up to date. Jean enters the birth of Clara, Tony enters the date of her engagement to Grünlich. Later she will record the dissolution of the marriage. At one level of its narrative identity, *Buddenbrooks* is a chronicle of family life, and its chronicling mode overlaps with the self-chronicling consciousness of the Buddenbrooks. The moments of precise temporal and spatial placing, coupled with the narrative mode that implicates us in the family consciousness, all give us a powerful sense of the truthful and undisputed presence of a whole way of life.

Here it is worth reflecting briefly on the novel's title, because it summarizes so many devices inherent in that rhetorical acknowledgment of a substantial world that so richly informs the novel's opening. The title, of course, names the family. But it names them, in the original German, without the definite article—not "die Buddenbrooks," but simply "Buddenbrooks." In German the omission of the definite article in this kind of context implies a degree of familiarity, even intimacy, with the family in question. In this sense, almost literally before we have started reading the novel, we find ourselves in a position of implied involvement with the family. And, as we have already seen, that register continues to dominate in the exposition and expresses itself in a number of tiny, but important, linguistic details.

Certain things about the family we are told but many more we simply have to pick up as we go along. It is as though the world of the novel has not been called into being for our benefit: it has been there all along; we simply happen to have called in, and hence we must take for granted what we do not yet understand. The narrative voice seems frequently content to take its cue from the characters. In regard to one particularly splendid housewarming gift that has been sent by Jean's father-in-law, Lebrecht Kröger, we learn that he is always the soul of generosity and elegance. Jean describes him as "aristocratic! generous! a cavalier à la mode" (I, 2, 10). One page later, Lebrecht's arrival is described: "Lebrecht Kröger, the cavalier à la mode, a tall distinguished figure, still wore his hair lightly powdered, but was fashionably dressed. In his velvet waistcoat two rows of jeweled buttons sparkled" (11). Many years later the modest disturbance that is the extent of Lübeck's participation in the mood of the 1848 Revolution shatters Lebrecht's world:

> *"Canaille!"* said Lebrecht Kröger in a cold and contemptuous voice. He had arrived in his carriage. The tall, distinguished figure of the cavalier à la mode began, under normal circumstances, to be bowed down under the burden of his eighty years; but today he stood quite erect. . . . In his black velvet waistcoat two rows of jeweled buttons sparkled. (IV, 3, 145)

The repetition of the detailed physical description in this passage is unmistakable, and it is, of course, utterly characteristic of that concern for continuity which informs the lives depicted and the novel itself. Lebrecht Kröger wears the same kind of waistcoat for his important public appearances, and the narrator's text records the fact. But the reference to the "cavalier à la mode" is particularly intriguing, not least because the epithet was applied originally to Lebrecht not by the narrator but by one of the characters. It is almost as though the narrator has borrowed the term from the characters; the fictional figures and not the recounter of the fiction have made the running. Indeed, their epithet is the one that supplies the old man's epitaph. Lebrecht is scandalized by the signs of social unrest he witnesses. A casually flung stone finds its way through the window of his carriage and strikes him a blow on the chest. Though not violent, the blow, together with the old man's fury, is enough to cause his death. Jean helps his father-in-law from the carriage, but it is too late: "Lebrecht Kröger, the cavalier à la mode, was with his forefathers" (IV, 4, 154). The characters' leitmotiv—Lebrecht as "cavalier à la mode"—is allowed to have the last word.

8

Narrative Technique:
The Inner Realm

In the preceding chapters I have highlighted some of the many occasions on which, by a variety of devices, the narrator pays tribute to the sheer solidity of that bourgeois realm that is the Buddenbrook habitat. Indeed, at times the narrator seems so to ally his voice with the outwardly perceivable form of familial and social recurrences that the inner life is a realm that can only be guessed at. Yet this, of course, is only part of the truth, for even in part I we are given glimpses of the inner life, often thanks to the device known as free indirect speech (or, as it is known in German, *erlebte Rede*).[1] In this narrative maneuver the pronouns and tenses are held in the mode of traditional narrative register (third person, past tense), yet certain other signals (such as reference to temporal or spatial co-ordinates—"today," or "here") make clear that the narrative report is, in fact, a transcription of the character's consciousness.

An extended example of this maneuver is found in part I when Christian makes himself sick through overeating. Grabow, the family doctor, is at hand and is able to reassure the anxious mother that there is nothing serious amiss; a light diet, apparently, will soon correct matters. And then we eavesdrop on the doctor's thoughts:

Dr. Grabow smiled to himself, his expression tolerant, a little melancholy even. Oh, he would eat again, the young man! He would live like all his kind. He would, like his forefathers, relatives, and acquaintances, spend his days sitting and would in between consume choice things, heavy and good things four times a day. . . . Well, may God be merciful! He, Friedrich Grabow was not the one to overturn the life-style of all these decent, prosperous, and comfortable merchant families. . . . That breadcrumbed ham with Charlotte sauce today had been, damn it all, wonderfully delicate. (I, 7, 25–26)

All but the first sentence of this passage is in free indirect speech. Whereas the essential linguistic signature is allied to traditional narrative (third person, imperfect tense), certain turns of phrase—"may God be merciful," "damn it all," "today"—reveal the present consciousness of the mind we are listening to. Clearly it is not the narrator who thinks that the "ham . . . today had been, damn it all, wonderfully delicate," but Dr. Grabow.

As the novel unfolds, this form of inward narration becomes more and more important precisely as later generations of Buddenbrooks become more and more introspective—and the narrator follows every twist and turn of their uneasy, problematic thought processes. Although the dimension of disturbance is not yet urgently present in part I, the potential, however understatedly, is there, waiting to be tapped. Admittedly, Dr. Grabow's reactions in the just-cited example are benign in this regard. As a medical man, he knows that, in all good conscience, he should warn these bourgeois families about the unhealthiness of their way of life. But he does not do so, not least because he too had enjoyed the food greatly. Dr. Grabow, then, does not seek to "overturn the life-style of all these decent, prosperous, and comfortable merchant families."

Later in the novel, however, subversive thoughts, thoughts that do aim to "overturn the life-style," make themselves heard. At the beginning of part II Jean is committing to the family chronicle the report of a recent and happy event; his wife, Elisabeth, has given birth to a little girl to be named Clara. Initially the narrator uses direct speech to report what Jean writes ("he wrote: 'Today, the 14th April 1838 . . .'"), but then he modulates into free indirect speech:

> It cannot be denied that the Consul felt the urge, after one or the other sentence, to call a halt, to put the pen aside, and to go and see his wife or to call in at the office. But how so? Did he grow so swiftly tired of communing with his creator and preserver? What a betrayal of Him, of the Lord, were he now to cease writing. . . . No, no. (II, 1, 38–39)

So Jean continues writing. When he has finished, he browses through the family chronicle. Many minor incidents are reported—childhood accidents, ailments, and so on—but there are also passages of emotion, of intense feeling such as Jean has just committed to paper, creating an undertow of a different order from the chronicling of the outward occasions of family life. At this stage of the family's existence, the moments of impassioned inwardness coexist with and do not supplant the essential solidity and efficiency of bourgeois life. In the spirit of the family mottoes, the Lord provides for the Buddenbrooks; moreover, the contribution that they themselves make to their own well-being is one that allows them to sleep well at night. But for later generations, a gulf will form between the individual conscience and the demands of practical living. That renegade inwardness will express itself through free indirect speech and sometimes by interior monologue.

One of the most sustained and striking examples of free indirect speech is Thomas's agonizing over whether to buy the Pöppenrade harvest. Maiboom the farmer is, as Thomas knows, pressed for money and prepared to come down in price and to sell the crop before it is harvested. Whoever buys such a crop is taking a risk, and that risk to the buyer depresses the price. The buyer handsomely profits if the crop turns out well but suffers a considerable financial loss if it fails. Thomas is caught in an agony of indecision. On the one hand, he feels he should say no, because the exploitativeness and riskiness of the deal ill becomes a Buddenbrook; little sound sleep is to be had after such transactions. On the other hand, he senses that this deal is one that would suit the Hagenströms; they, and the kinds of business to which they are attuned, are symptomatic of the new age that has little room for the Buddenbrooks and what they stand for. Thomas's thoughts, couched in free indirect speech, undermine any notion of the fulfillment vouchsafed by and in the practical world:

> Was Thomas Buddenbrook a businessman, a man of action, or a brooding dreamer?
> Ah yes, that was the question; for a long time, ever since he could think for himself, that had been the kind of question he asked! Life was hard, and the business world, in its ruthless and unsentimental processes, was an image of the totality of life. Did Thomas Buddenbrook stand with both feet firmly planted in the hard practicality of life, as his fathers had done? (VIII, 4, 370)

At the most immediate level, Thomas's anguish has to do with matters of business and economics, with the kind of transaction that is or is not appropriate to the Buddenbrook firm. But the crisis—for such it is—cannot be contained within these bounds. Ultimately at stake is Thomas Buddenbrook's person and whether he can cope with the stresses and strains of living in the practical world. Similar questions, couched in similar terms and framed within a similar narrative rhetoric of intense inwardness, recur later when Thomas by chance comes across a book of philosophy that he takes to the summerhouse to browse through:

> He felt the incomparable satisfaction of watching a powerfully superior mind take hold of life, of this strong, cruel and mocking thing called life, in order to subjugate and condemn it . . . the satisfaction of the sufferer who, impelled by shame and bad conscience, always kept his suffering hidden from the coldness and the hardness of life and who suddenly receives from the hand of a great and wise man the essential and solemn justification for his suffering at the hands of the world. (X, 5, 510–11)

Narrative Technique: The Inner Realm

To express such moments of intense inwardness Mann employs a narrative mode that at times modulates from free indirect speech into full interior monologue (in the present tense with first-person pronouns): "Have I ever hated life, this pure, cruel, and strong life? Folly and misunderstanding! I have only hated myself—because I could not bear it. But I love you" (X, 5, 513). Clearly such a narrative mode is expressly conceived to bring us close to the stressful mind, to make us understand not only the urgency and the eloquence of the insights glimpsed but also their central concepts and implications.

Similar devices for making radical inwardness articulate and accessible are also found in connection with Hanno. Particularly noteworthy is the moment in which the four-and-a-half-year-old Hanno is described at play. The passage does not, in fact, give us many details of the games Hanno played but tells us of the philosophical significance of his childhood joys. The narrative technique is not free indirect speech; Hanno is too young to be able to formulate such perceptions of human joy and pain. Instead, the narrative voice offers its own formulation of the worth and dignity of Hanno's joys and, by the insistent, impassioned use of the pronoun *wir,* "we," demands our assent to the truthfulness of what is being said.

We have by now come a long way from the use of the pronoun *man* ("one") in the opening pages of the novel, whereby we were aligned with the corporate presence and consciousness of the family. Now we are asked to acknowledge truths that are radically subversive of practical adult living:

Above all the pure, strong, ardent, chaste, still uncontaminated and unintimidated fantasy of those blissful years in which life still holds back from tampering with us, in which neither duty nor guilt dares to lay a finger upon us, in which we may see, hear, laugh, wonder, and dream without the world demanding services from us. . . . Alas, not much longer, and with crude tyranny everything will descend upon us in order to assault us, to drill, to rack, to trim, to ruin us. (VII, 8, 342–43)

The narrative passion here is unmistakable. What is being talked about is not simply a psychological condition, a childhood idyll before the demands of adult life make themselves felt. The narrator also invokes a philosophical drama in which the soul's innocence is celebrated before the deforming, brutalizing inroads of practical living make themselves felt. As so often in this novel, philosophical and psychological arguments merge in powerful narrative meditation on the inner life.

The climactic expressions of Hanno's intense inwardness emerge when the narrative voice seeks to convey the force and eloquence of the music he makes. It is in music rather than in discursive thought that Hanno is at his most articulate. In passages of remarkable prose Thomas Mann contrives to suggest both the particular idiom of Hanno's music—it savors, unmistakably, Wagnerian chromaticism—and the philosophical drama of physical obstacles and metaphysical yearnings. Mann uses a narrative technique that mediates between description of the musical argument and, by means of rhetorical questions, a kind of free indirect speech whereby a self-explicating consciousness is attributed to the music, above all to its overwhelming, orgiastic climax. Consider these excerpts from a passage in which the narrative voice voluptuously savors the resolution of a dissonance:

> It was an entirely simple motif that he introduced, a trifle, the fragment of a nonexistent melody, a figure of one and a half bars, and when he announced it first as a single voice in a low register and with a strength one would not have thought him capable of, as though it were to be proclaimed by trombones in authoritative unison as the fountainhead and source of everything that was to come—there was no way of telling what was intended. But when he repeated it in the treble, harmonized in sound colors of matt silver, it turned out that it essentially consisted of one single resolution, a longing and painful movement down from one key into another. . . . And now began troubled movements, a restless, syncopated coming and going. . . . A fermata ensued, and silence. And behold, suddenly there was, in sound colors of matt silver, the first motif again, quite soft, this pitiful invention. . . . Then there arose an immense tumult. . . . What was happening? What was being ex-

pressed? Were here fearful obstacles being overcome, dragons slain, rocks scaled, rivers crossed, flames walked through? . . . And then began a swelling upwards, a slow, unstoppable intensification, a chromatic striving upwards of wild, irresistible longing. . . . And it came, it could be withheld no longer, the spasms of longing could be no longer prolonged. . . . The solution, the resolution, the fulfillment, total bliss broke through. . . . It was the motif, the first motif, that sounded forth! And what now began was a celebration, a triumph, an untrammeled orgy of this figure. (XI, 2, 586–88)

The narrative perspective here aligns us with a putative community of Hanno's hearers, just as earlier in the novel we are implicated in the collective responses of the Buddenbrook Thursday gathering. Hanno's music states the first motif with a force that "one would not have thought him capable of." The pronoun "one" has a corporate range of reference; we are made to share in the drama of this music, to discover it with the narrator, to respond to it as it unfolds. The first motif "turned out" to be a single resolution. The return of that motif is experienced, and celebrated, as a sudden revelation: "And behold, suddenly there was. . . ." The narrator leaves us in no doubt as to the drama and passion inherent in Hanno's playing and to the expressive power derived from the structural and harmonic argument of the music. We join with the narrative voice in searching for the meaning of the desperate quest expressed in the turbulent sounds: "What was happening? What was being expressed?" And the release, when it comes, is conveyed through a veritable cascade of nouns: "The solution, the resolution, the fulfillment, total bliss broke through."

The narrator's account conveys, and demands that we share in, the torrential intensity of Hanno's music. Moreover, the passage, in a quite masterly way, mixes technical terms of musical analysis both with a psychological vocabulary of emotional craving and release and with concepts derived from philosophical discourse having to do with being and nothingness—*Nichts, wesentlich, Urstoff*. In musicological terms, the composition is manifestly an immature exercise in the manner of the *Liebestod* from the end of Richard Wagner's *Tristan und Isolde*—immature in the precise sense that sophisticated devices of modulation and harmony are used ultimately in the service of an end-less milking of the simple motif for its yield of orgiastic bliss. The music culminates in an orgy of that initial phrase which is described as a "trifle." The German word is *ein Nichts,* literally "a nothing." It is this nothing that is the primal matter of Hanno's statement, that is the "Urstoff und Ausgang alles Kommenden"; the final, unmistakably sexual, release is an orgy in celebration of the nothing. The inwardness that in Hanno's grandfather was an intensity of religious feeling, that in his father became a reverie about the brutality of living and the possibilities for a kind of secular immortality, has become in Hanno the radical and incurable wish not to live. Jean and Thomas had found language to be the vessel and medium of their illumination; with Hanno it is music. Narratively, Thomas Mann manages to find the musicological registers appropriate for the expression of this intense inwardness.

The spectrum of narrative discourse starts with the abundantly detailed cataloging of the outer world via the understated, self-effacing gesture of simply eavesdropping on the characters' linguistic behavior patterns and extends to the account, whether through indirect speech, free indirect speech, or interior monologue, of the texture, feel, and substance of the characters' inwardness. Thomas Mann's narrative moves flexibly from outward to inward not so much to play one realm off the other but mainly to explore their interconnectedness—even where the gulf between them would seem unbridgeable.

With his unemphatic narration of the opening part of *Budden-brooks*—unemphatic precisely in that the narrator, by not explaining what is self-evident to the characters, makes the reader assent to the self-evidentness of the bourgeois world—Thomas Mann implies that the workings of any given social world are anchored not simply in certain obvious facts and events but also in the values, ideas, concepts, symbols, and assumptions of the time. These are so much second na-ture to the members of that society that they are not spelled out, not made explicit and reflected on. Mann develops precisely the appro-priate narrative register to express this set of operative processes. Successive generations of Buddenbrooks come to find it increasingly difficult to take the outward world and its value scale for granted, because inwardly they are increasingly at variance with these values. To them the self-explanatory is no longer that; it needs explanation, and the explanation is only imperfectly forthcoming. The quest for explanations and values characterizes their inwardness; it is, then, both a psychological and a philosophical condition. Mann constantly makes us attend to that interlocking of philosophy and psychology.

9

Inwardness

The first instances of inwardness that challenge the practical outer world of the Buddenbrooks are religious in character. Gotthold's letter, which is quoted in full in chapter 10 of part I, appeals for charity by invoking the promptings of the Christian conscience: "I must say to you that the way in which you by your obstinacy are widening the gulf which, may the Lord be merciful, exists between us, is a sin for which you will at some time have to answer most grievously before God's judgment throne" (I, 10, 33). Old Johann at this point has little difficulty in getting his son Jean to resist such blandishments, but, increasingly, religious sentiment comes to play a central role in Jean's life.

Part II opens with Jean recording in the family chronicle his gratitude for the birth of his daughter Clara, but the report of the event merges into expressions of intense religious adoration: "After three pages the Consul wrote an 'Amen,' but the pen sped onward, sped with its scratching sound over many a page, and wrote of the precious spring which restores the weary wanderer, of the Saviour's holy wounds pouring blood" (II, 1, 38). The key notions here—weariness on the one hand and delicious, thirst-quenching comfort on the other—recur, in manifold variation, throughout the novel. At this point in the story though, it would seem that Jean is the first Budden-brook to know an experience that calls efficient, successful living into question. But this proves not to be the case. Having written his im-passioned reflections on God's mercy, Jean begins to browse through the family chronicle and eventually comes across some entirely aston-ishing remarks written in his father's hand. Old Johann was married for a year to the daughter of a merchant from Bremen named Jose-phine. She died in giving birth to Gotthold. Johann, as the dynastic requirements dictate, reported this fact in the family chronicle. But he went further than that. The chronicle entry modulated into a diary entry. The impersonal voice of familial continuity became dislodged by the personal tones of unspeakable anguish at the destruction of his dearly beloved wife by this ruthless baby.

Here we begin to understand that there are other motivations be-hind the old man's implacable resistance to Gotthold's pleading. We also perceive that even the unproblematic Johann has known depri-vation of such intensity that the everyday world in which he and his second wife, Antoinette, appear so utterly anchored never quite counts for as much as it once did:

> Johann Buddenbrook seemed genuinely and bitterly to have hated this new life from the moment when its first bold movements caused the mother dreadful pain—to have hated it up to the moment when it was born, healthy and vigorous, while Josephine, her bloodless head buried deep into the pillows, died—and never to have forgiven this unscrupulous intruder, who grew up strong and carefree, for having murdered his mother. (II, 1, 41)

The key terms in this passage—"bold," "healthy," "lively," "unscru-pulous," "strong," "carefree"—will dominate the later stages of the novel, because, remarkably, when we are allowed to hear the full mea-sure of Thomas's and Hanno's loathing of the world, the terms that frame their inwardness will be very similar to old Johann's impas-sioned account in the family chronicle of his irreparable loss.

At the moment of death, old Johann registers primarily the strangeness of his ceasing to be a Buddenbrook. It would seem that, in radical contrast to his great-grandson Hanno, who spends all too much of his life in love with easeful death, he has not given death a thought before it, as it were, arrives to claim him. But old Johann is vouchsafed a glimpse of that metaphysical reflection which later generations will come to know all too well:

> He was not thinking a great deal, he merely looked back constantly and with a gentle shake of the head on his life and life in general, which now seemed to him so distant and strange, this unnecessarily clamorous toing and froing, in whose midst he had stood, which had imperceptibly withdrawn from him and which now sounded distantly to his surprised harkening ear. (II, 4, 52–53)

Once again, the notion, twice mentioned, of life having become strangely distant ("fern," "in der Ferne"), of being noisy, empty tumult ("dieses überflüssig geräuschvolle Getümmel"), points us forward to Hanno's strangely lucid reverie at the crisis point of his illness. Moreover, the narrator is explicit in telling us that old Johann thought back over his life and *life in general* ("das Leben im allgemeinen"). Death has begun to awaken metaphysical questionings in even one of the most stalwart servants of the practical world.

Much later in the novel, another moment of death brings into focus the summons of inwardness, of metaphysical reflection. Thomas witnesses the death of Gotthold, and he ponders on the meaning of that life with its central act of rebellion against the Buddenbrook ethos in the name of love. He wonders if old Johann was not right in one sense about his firstborn—Gotthold was ruthless and single-minded rather than reflective and sophisticated. Thomas thinks about his uncle because of the possible bond between them. Thomas, too, fell in love with somebody unsuitable by Buddenbrook standards (Anna of the flower shop,[1] who becomes Frau Iwersen, and whose silent grief at Thomas's death goes virtually unremarked by the family). But Thomas did not stick to his guns in the way that Uncle Gotthold did.

Inwardness

For Thomas, something more was—and is—involved than simple conformism; it is rather an ironically knowing observance of the rules of the game, because, so Thomas has concluded, whatever one does on the earth, one is playing a role, one is acting "as if":

> The sense of poetry was lacking in you, although you were brave enough to love and to marry in defiance of your father's commandment. . . . Oh, we too are sufficiently traveled and cultivated to perceive perfectly well that the limits set to our ambition, viewed from outside and from above, are but narrow and pitiful. But everything on earth is only a metaphor, Uncle Gotthold! Did you not know that one can be a great man even in a small town? (V, 4, 215)

The notion that the limited world of practical living can be tolerated because it is merely one contingent—and therefore not ultimately binding—version of what one might be and do is symptomatic of Thomas's ironic distance from Lübeck and Buddenbrook values. Precisely that distance is the measure of his reflective, questioning, and questing inwardness. Yet at the same time, he knows that the particular world in which he finds himself is the stage on which he has to act out his life, that its rules are the ones by which he has to play, and he is dismissive of both Christian and Hanno for not even attempting to heed the rules.

Thomas's irony is the index of his need to keep at arm's length those alien rules that will finally destroy him. Initially, it is the controllable irony, the presence of manageable, unparalyzing inwardness that allows Thomas to be a successful and enterprising businessman. In an explicit echo of the moment at Gotthold's deathbed, the narrator comments on Thomas's character as follows:

> And so he had wit enough to make the saying about the merely symbolic significance of all human activity into one of his central beliefs, and so he placed everything that he could call his own by way of will, ability, enthusiasm, and active drive in the service of the little community within whose confines his name was one of the

first—and in the service of the name and family arms he had inherited. . . . Wit enough, at one and the same time, to smile at and to
take seriously his ambition, within this small realm, to achieve
greatness and significance. (VI, 7, 282)

This is a wonderful moment of portraiture, for the narrator joins psychological and philosophical concerns to render for us the inner landscape of this man's selfhood. Thomas Buddenbrook knows that
Lübeck is *a* world and not *the* world. He is able to reflect on both, on
the links and differences between them. In the course of the novel the
differences prevail over the links, gradually sundering Thomas from
any sustained or fulfilling belief in his whole public and social role
within the small, indeed confining, world of his forefathers.

It is a measure of the deepening crisis that when Thomas next
formulates his perceptions about the symbolic nature of human existence, he does so in terms of an almost Manichaean horror at the
material world. He concludes that the "real" things in his life—the
splendid new house in the Fischergrube that they have just moved
into; the everyday dealings and contracts that make up the life of a
businessman; his recent election, in preference to his great rival Hermann Hagenström, as senator—are but empty emblems, bric-a-brac
and devalued currency, none of which satisfies the deepest needs of the
human personality. The passage is a long one, and I quote in excerpts:

I greatly looked forward to all this, but this anticipation was, as
always, the best part, for good things come always too late. . . . And
when they come, the good and longed-for things, ponderous and
overdue, they are weighed down by all the trivial, disturbing, irri-
tating trappings, by all the dust of reality. . . . I have in the last few
days been thinking often of a Turkish proverb that I read some-
where: "when the house is finished, then death comes." Well, it does
not have to be death exactly. But descent . . . falling-off . . . the beginning of the end. . . . "Senator" and "house" are external
things. . . . I know that often outward, visible, touchable signs and
symbols of good fortune and success only appear when in truth
everything is already in the process of decline. (VII, 6, 337–38)

The last sentence is particularly devastating in its implications. Thomas makes a distinction between the outwardness of symbols ("die äusseren, sichtbarlichen und greifbaren Zeichen und Symbole des Glückes") and the truth ("in Wahrheit"). The symbol is, then, little better than a sham; the outward, physical, touchable world is a lie. Thomas knows that he dare not think these thoughts of disparaging inwardness for too long, that he must override them with notions of the dignity and value of practical activity in the material world. But the dark, bitter truth will not allow itself to be banished forever.

A mere four pages later we read, in a passage from which I have previously quoted, of the bliss of Hanno's childhood games. It is a bliss related to the fact that fantasy prevails totally; the world does not yet demand any allegiance from us. In describing this psychological condition the narrator makes frequent use of the first-person plural pronoun, in effect asking for our assent, both psychologically and philosophically, to the happiness of a condition beyond the blight of worldliness: "those happy years in which . . . we may see, hear, laugh, wonder, and dream without the world demanding services from us" (VII, 8, 342). Here we recognize that the eroding inwardness glimpsed in Thomas will take complete possession of Hanno, sapping utterly his will to live.

Thomas's attempt to deny the renegade voice within him is radically disturbed when he is confronted with the chance to buy the Pöppenrade crop before it has been harvested. In terms of the psychological issue of the novel the passage explores Thomas's divided self:

> Was he a practical man or a tenderhearted dreamer?
> Ah, he had put this question to himself a thousand times, and he had answered it—in strong and self-confident hours—one way, and—in weary hours—another way. But he was too perceptive and honest not to have to admit that he was a mixture of both. (VIII, 4, 370–71)

This psychological mechanism at the heart of the "decline of a family" feeds into the philosophical issue, according to which all the scrupulous, compassionate, thoughtful impulses of mankind are irremediably opposed to the sheer brutality of the life force. We read that in many sleepless nights "full of disgust, and hurt beyond all comfort, he had revolted against the ugly and shameless hardness of life!" (370). The spirit and the conceptual patterning of this experience reach all the way back to old Johann's entry in the family chronicle about the brutality with which baby Gotthold destroyed his mother's life during childbirth. Part of the horror that runs through Thomas's debate with himself derives from the particular character of the proposed business transaction. In all kinds of ways, he feels himself disgusted: it is an exploitative deal in that it takes advantage of the farmer's urgent need to raise money; it is a high-risk, speculative transaction with the chance of winning or losing a significant sum of money. Above all, it seems to demand a degree of moral and financial sangfroid, even callousness, that Thomas cannot muster. The brutality of Life with a capital "L," of life as a philosophical concept, merges with the quite particular socioeconomic form of life as it confronts Thomas Buddenbrook:

> Life was hard, and business life was in its ruthless and unsentimental workings an image of the grandeur and totality of life. . . .
>
> He recalled the impression that the catastrophe of '66 had made on him. . . . He had lost a large sum of money . . . ah, that was not the most intolerable thing about it. Rather, he had had to experience at first hand and in full measure the cruel brutality of business life, in which all kind, gentle, and compassionate feelings withdrew before the raw, naked, dominant instinct of self-preservation. (VIII, 4, 370)

Yet however much anguished self-examination the Pöppenrade harvest deal causes Thomas and however profound the enforced reckoning with his own weakness may be, he persists in denying what he has come to know about himself and the world. Hanno particularly is on the receiving end of this willed unreflectiveness. Because of his "sense of the family, this inherited and acquired, both backward- and forward-looking, piety in respect of the intimate history of his house"

(X, 2, 483), Thomas deludes himself into thinking that the simple existence of Hanno as heir to the Buddenbrook legacy justifies visions of future "enterprise, practical and confident work" (484). These terms we have met before—"Tüchtigkeit, praktisch[e] und unbefangen[e] Arbeit." In the moments of inwardness, they always stand for the tribute that the practical, efficient world demands of its servants.

In a wonderfully vivid cameo, we witness the interplay of Thomas's wishful thinking and Hanno's unnerving ability to see through his father's self-deception. Sometimes Thomas has to make duty visits in the town. Gerda dislikes accompanying him and frequently invents some excuse. In this case, Thomas takes Hanno with him, hoping, in these moments of publicly representative activity, to inculcate into his son the values he will later need to espouse: "self-confidence . . . , ruthlessness, and a simple feeling for practical life" (X, 2, 491). But it does not work that way, for Hanno knows and sees too much. He sees though his father's act (we have already noted how insistently the metaphor of the actor is applied to Thomas in the later years of his life). Moreover—and this is the crucial point—the rhetoric of seeing, of knowing deeply, more deeply and more truthfully than is good for one, is urgently present in the moments of decisive inwardness. Hanno watches Thomas enacting the symbolic role of his public existence, and he knows that his father is only going through the motions:

> But little Johann saw more than he was supposed to see, and his eyes, those shy, golden-brown eyes with their blueish shadows, observed all too well. He saw not only the assured friendliness that his father extended to everybody, he also saw—saw it with a strange, tormenting sharpness of vision—what a toll it took of him to produce this manner. (X, 2, 490)

Hanno's insight into his father's weakness is, of course, insight into and recognition of his own terrible debility.

There are two further key moments that merit discussion. The weightiest is the experience Thomas has, seemingly by chance, when he comes upon a book of philosophy, which he takes to the summerhouse and reads. He responds to this experience with the intensity of someone vouchsafed a revelation. His reverie has two principal strands, both of which have previously been part of his awareness but now achieve a new eloquence and urgency. The first strand is the suffering of a sensitive and scrupulous spirit occasioned by the sheer brutality of life:

> He felt the incomparable satisfaction of watching a powerfully superior mind take hold of life, of this strong, cruel, and mocking thing called life, in order to subjugate it and condemn it . . . the satisfaction of the sufferer who, impelled by shame and bad conscience, always kept his suffering hidden from the coldness and the hardness of life and who suddenly receives from the hand of a great and wise man the essential and solemn justification for suffering at the hands of the world. (X, 5, 510.)

The key terms for coldness, hardness, cruelty (*stark, grausam, höhnisch, Kälte, Härte*, and so on) have all occurred before in the novel. They are almost the essential signature of Buddenbrook inwardness. Here they are challenged by the second strand of Thomas's musings in which he finds within himself an intense affirmation of life, even with its cruelty and indifference. That affirmation comes to him with all the authority of an epiphany: "And behold: suddenly it was as though the darkness were rent asunder before his eyes, as though the velvet wall of night split wide open and revealed an infinitely deep, eternal prospect of light" (512).

In Thomas's philosophical vision, the seeing deeply during moments of inwardness is manifestly endowed with religious authority. Thomas comes to realize that he will live on—not in his son Hanno, but in those who say "yes" fully to living in the world:

> Somewhere in the world a boy is growing up, well endowed and well formed, blessed with the ability to develop his gifts, growing straight and untroubled, pure, cruel, serene, one of those beings the sight of whom intensifies the happiness of the happy and drives the unhappy one to despair:—That is my son. That I will be, soon. (513)

70

The two central strands in Thomas's experience of philosophical illumination contradict one another, but they do so in a complementary
way, for common to both is a belief in the harshness and brutality of
life. In the first set of reflections Thomas finds himself confirmed in
his suffering, in the torment he has undergone by trying to make himself believe in and serve the brutal mechanisms of living. In the second,
however, he reverses the evaluative responses; he concludes that he
has hated not life itself but his own weakness, and that now the prospect of his death promises release from the aberration that is the individual self. In merging with the untrammeled swell of living energy,
Thomas will find his true existence after death in those who live their
lives with no separate, individuated, reflective consciousness but
rather as embodiments of the life force itself, unself-conscious, proud,
strong.

Two points should be stressed about this extraordinary and intense moment of philosophical inwardness. The first is that Thomas
is not a professional philosopher; he does not argue with conceptual
rigor or logical clarity. In fact, he does not argue at all; rather, he
experiences the revelations "not in words and sequential thoughts but
in sudden, transporting illuminations of his inner self" (514). There is
no need for us to resolve Thomas's intuitions and glimpses into a coherent philosophical system. As Mann put it in his *Reflections of an
Unpolitical Man,* "One can think in the sense of a philosopher without
in the slightest following his sense; that means that one can use his
thoughts and yet in the process think in ways that he does not
intend."[2]

The second point is that this climactic point of inwardness does
not, in fact, change anything. It does not leave Thomas with insights
or values or principles with which he can better control and master
his life. The illumination fades without trace. Thomas returns to his
daily life and is worn down by it. On the instructions of his doctor,
he goes to Travemünde for a brief holiday. There he speaks to Tony of
his deep attachment to the sea. It is his last moment of inwardness,
and it does not suggest in any way that Thomas has retained insights
and perceptions from his meeting with the discourse of speculative
philosophy. His thoughts on the sea express an intense longing for

peace, and his mind plays on the contrast between the appeal of mountains and the appeal of the sea:

> The simplest [distinction] is that one clambers bravely around in the mountains while one rests quietly in the sand by the seashore. But I know the gaze with which one pays homage to the one or to the other. Self-confident, defiant, happy eyes that are full of enterprise, certainty, love of life wander from peak to peak; but on the immensity of the sea, that with this mystical and paralyzing fatalism sends its waves rolling up the shore, there rests, dreaming, a veiled, hopeless, and knowing glance, that somewhere once looked deep into tragic perplexities. (X, 6, 524)

Once again we hear the note of the thoughtfulness, the reflectiveness that looks deep into experience and emerges not with certainty, not with a life-affirming purpose, but with weariness, with a longing to join the infinite, unindividuated, simple oneness of the sea. Thomas's inwardness, his thinking, searching, and questioning, brings him ultimately to this overwhelming death wish.

Clearly we have to ask ourselves what the scenes exploring Thomas's moments of inner crisis and self-scrutiny amount to. And we must begin by recognizing that these moments of inwardness constantly suggest how psychological, theological, philosophical, and socioeconomic issues intermingle. Moreover—and this is a crucial point—certain features of that inner life, particularly the meeting with the book of philosophy, give the inner turmoil a certain representative status. The book Thomas comes across and reads is not identified in the novel, but it is in fact by Schopenhauer and forms part of his major work, *The World as Will and Representation*. Schopenhauer began publishing his magnum opus in 1819, but the mood of the times was profoundly out of sympathy with his somber view of human experience. By the mid-nineteenth century, however, he had come very much into fashion. Mann observed in the *Reflections of an Unpolitical Man,*

> Indeed, that find which Thomas Buddenbrook made in a dusty corner of his bookcase, only seemingly did he make it by chance; not

many years before, Europe, intellectual . . . Europe had made the same find. The pessimism of Arthur Schopenhauer prevailed, it was very much in fashion in European intellectual circles.[3]

There is, then, a measure of simple historical plausibility to the novel's assertion that Thomas could indeed have picked up cheaply part of what, by the time he comes to browse in it, has become a famous metaphysical system. But the "rightness" of his excursion into philosophy is more profound than that. Thomas's sense of revelation on reading Schopenhauer was that of a whole German generation in the 1860s. For Schopenhauer, the world is governed by a blind, ruthless life force that he calls the Will. The Will is essentially the principle of living matter finding means to serve its own ends—procreating, reproducing itself, generating living organisms. For Schopenhauer, all the finest promptings of humankind are necessarily offended by this monstrous and brutal energy, and suffer at every turn from its inescapable vitality and striving. The saint, the ascetic, the artist—these figures, in Schopenhauer's view, come as close as human beings can to denying the Will, to removing themselves from its clutches. Thereby they find as much wisdom and insight as are available to humankind. Schopenhauer's central doctrine, then, is a pessimistic one. Living is a mindless and brutal process, and quietism represents the highest human good.

Yet, as we have seen, Thomas Buddenbrook constantly reacts against the defeatism of such a worldview; with part of his being he wants to subscribe to vitalist, affirmatory thinking, to expressions of intense, untrammeled, unreflective living. That aspiration is, although Thomas at the time of his philosophical reverie can hardly know it, enshrined in the work of a contemporary: Friedrich Nietzsche. Mann comments at one point about Thomas, "Here was somebody thinking who, apart from Schopenhauer, had also read Nietzsche and who transposed the one experience into the other, and produced the strangest concoction of the two."[4] Nietzsche's writings, which are central to the temper of German and European culture in the last two and a half decades of the nineteenth century, are in a sense an answer to Schopenhauer. Nietzsche was profoundly indebted to Schopenhauer; they shared many basic premises, above all the key perception that the world was not informed by any higher purpose other than its own continued functioning, not animated by any sublime goal or aim (such as sustains Hegel's thinking, for example). Yet Nietzsche sought, on this barren ground, this world bereft of purpose and significance, to erect a philosophy that would say yes to life in the very teeth of its inherent unjustifiability. Nietzsche saw himself as providing a critique of those previous philosophical systems that had sought to invest the world with meaning and to make it part of some grandiose scheme of values. For Nietzsche, the lack of values, the lack of truth, the lack of redemption, the lack of significance had to be enough for humankind to live by—and to live abundantly, joyously. In his strange excursus into philosophy, Thomas Buddenbrook arrives at the unfocused yet eloquent interplay of the two philosophers whose voices very much chart the spiritual landscape of the German-speaking lands in the second half of the nineteenth century. He comes, in other words, however confusedly, however imperfectly, to think the thoughts of his age and culture. And in this sense, in a moment of intense and private inwardness, this problematic and troubled grain merchant from Lübeck comes to be representative of his age; paradoxically, the private, in its very repudiation of the public realm, yet expresses that public realm.

Thomas has not been trained in Schopenhauer's, Nietzsche's, or anyone else's philosophy. The processes of imprinting are incomparably more subtle and mediated than that; he has not visibly been conditioned by any obvious institutional pressures or authoritarian personalities to think the thoughts he does. Yet he is not free from the inroads of the world around him. When he strains every mental and moral nerve to find out the truth about himself, about how he has lived and about how he should live, the illuminations that come to him do so with the force of personal, existential truths. There is no arbiter other than the self that he is. There is, in this sense, a real dignity to his risk taking, to his desperate, lacerating pursuit of the truth. Yet the truth he finds is essentially his own dilemma writ large; moreover, that truth does him no good, it does not solve anything.

And, as we have just seen, it is not even inalienably and irreducibly his; it is part of the discourse of his age. We now touch the heart of Mann's insight in regard to the inwardness that informs *Budden-brooks*. At one level, the inwardness bears the imprint of the out-wardness of its time and place; there is no private, protected inner self proof against the inroads of the tendencies and pressures of the cor-porate world outside it. Both adherence to the norms of one's socio-cultural conditioning and dissent from them are in large measure conditioned responses. There is no unconditioned—and therefore un-conditional—cognition available to men and women. Human beings are thought as well as thinking. The signs, terms, concepts, and expressions within which they live, move, and have their being are never exclusively theirs but are part of the corporate discourses that form their world. Even so, *Buddenbrooks* does not allow us to see the characters as merely imprinted, conditioned creatures; it makes us rec-ognize that their quest for meaning, their need to know and articulate what goes on inside them and around them, has a measure of dignity and creativity that stands as a genuine human achievement.

This issue of conditioning and creativity brings me to Hanno and the modes of his inwardness. Whereas Thomas, in his own way, does try to both join and resist the brutal world, Hanno simply recoils from it altogether. (In this sense, he is contrasted with his friend Kai, who has all Hanno's sensitivity and aversion to the stresses and strains of efficient social living but also has a fierce determination to live his own life on his own terms, whatever the struggle involved. Kai enshrines the possibility that sensitivity and courage can coexist.) The chapter that describes Hanno helplessly exposed to the pressures of institu-tional life is the novel's longest; it amounts to an impassioned denun-ciation of the horror of what schooling can do to a young person. The school, of course, is an institution intensely implicated in the process of socialization, of imprinting young people with certain values that will inform the rest of their lives. Hence, the school is a symbolic nexus for the life of the society at large. Thomas Mann's verdict is about as devastating as is Dickens's on Mr. Gradgrind's establishment in *Hard Times*.[5] If, for Thomas Buddenbrook, the life of a businessman is paradigmatic of the brutality of life in general, for his son school has that same exemplary force.

Hanno's weakness is of a piece with his critical insight, with his ability to perceive all the manifold mechanisms of vanity and self-assertion at work. One example can stand for many. Most of the teachers are humorless, authoritarian monsters for whom drill is the only teaching method and learning by heart the only kind of study. But in the fourth period of Hanno's day, the class is taught English by one Herr Modersohn, who, as the boys know only too well, is on a trial contract at the school. He cannot keep order and the pupils tease him unmercifully. At one joke Hanno joins in the general laughter, and Herr Modersohn singles him out for punishment, because the weak, as Hanno bitterly reflects, have no option but to pick on the weak:

> [Hanno] saw inside him as well. Hanno Buddenbrook was almost the only one whom Herr Modersohn knew by name, and he used that fact to take him constantly to task, to give him extra essays as punishment, and to tyrannize him. He knew Buddenbrook from the other pupils because he had distinguished himself by his gentle behavior, and he exploited this gentleness to wield his authority constantly, which he never dared to do with regard to the loud and insolent boys. On earth even pity is destroyed by spite, thought Hanno. I take no part in tormenting and exploiting you, Candidate Modersohn, because I find it brutal, ugly, and common, and how do you repay me? But that is the way it is, it will always be like this, he thought, and fear and nausea rose within him. And that I, moreover, have to see through you with that ghastly clarity! (XI, 2, 578)

As so often before, we must note here the modulation into direct quotation from the character's consciousness. Again, the key terms make themselves heard—"brutal," "ugly," "fear"—compounded by the familiar notion of seeing deeply, of seeing through the pretensions of daily living. The day at school wonderfully interweaves social and institutional issues with psychological concerns (Hanno's disablingly clear perceptions of the mechanisms of vanity and weakness) and with philosophical discourses (suffering, fear, insight). Thomas sees

through the practical world but manages—at terrible cost to himself—
to serve it. Hanno knows only the weariness and shame that haunt his
existence in the social world.

The only time Hanno asserts himself is when he improvises at the
piano. There he takes hold of the weariness, disgust, and fear that are
at the center of his inwardness and expresses them with all the volup-
tuousness and passion of a sexual consummation. At the end of his
disastrous day in school, he improvises at the piano. There is no au-
dience; he is playing only for himself—and us. His playing culminates
in the fanatical, orgiastic celebration of that trifle, that nonmelody,
that *nothing*, with which it begins. When, at the beginning of the next
chapter, we read, "The course of typhoid is as follows" (XI, 3, 588),
we can, given the death wish that Hanno expresses so overwhelmingly
in his music, hardly doubt that the unnamed victim is he. By virtue of
the term *Auflösung*, which in music means "resolution," the disease
seems related to the music we have heard, for *Auflösung* also means
"decay," "dissolution." The first motif of Hanno's improvisation "essentially consisted of one single resolution" ("im wesentlichen aus einer einzigen Auflösung bestand" [XI, 2, 586]), and therefore that
motif is nothing but "dissolution." Although the bulk of the typhoid
chapter is clinical in tone and import, in the final paragraph we are
told that typhoid may be less a specific disease with a precise symptomatology than "quite simply a form of dissolution ["Auflösung"],
the garb of death itself, which could equally well appear in some other
guise, and against which there is no remedy" (XI, 3, 590–91). The
ominous noun makes the link with Hanno's music.

This paragraph moves us totally away from the clinical registers
with which the chapter began. The crisis in the disease is a moment
that is metaphysical rather than physical in character. It is a moment
that summarizes all those moments of inwardness we have been discussing, going right back to the early stages of the novel, to Johann's
reflections on the loss of his beloved Josephine. For the last time, the
key concepts are heard—the bright, fresh, scornful, brutal processes
of living and the promise of release from them, of peace beyond their
reach and sway. Hanno hears the call of life beckoning him to return;

we know the answer he, from the center of his inwardness, will give:

> Impervious and fresh, this voice will reach the spirit on the strange hot path along which he is walking and which leads into the shadows, into coolness and peace. The person will prick up his ears and will hear this bright, cheerful, a little scornful admonition to turn round, to turn back. . . . If there is a great surge of emotion within him, like a sense of cowardly betrayal of a duty, of shame, of renewed energy, of courage and joy, of love and attachment to the mocking, colorful and brutal mechanism that he has left behind him; then, however far he may have strayed along the strange, hot path, he will turn back and live. But if he shudders in fear and revulsion on hearing the voice of life, if this memory, this cheerful, challenging sound causes him to shake his head and to stretch out a forbidding hand behind him and to flee further along the path which has opened up before him as release . . . no, then it is clear, then he will die. (XI, 3, 590f.)

This vivid and eloquent passage describes a moment in which the individual self is confronted by Hamlet's supreme question, "To be or not to be." It is a moment of existential decision making, and that existential dimension generalizes the implications of the passage, extending them beyond the symptomatology of a particular disease. We notice that, even in the six "clinical" paragraphs, the victim is sometimes described as the sufferer or the patient (*der Kranke* or *der Patient*), which is what one would expect. But on two occasions, at the beginning of the second and fourth paragraphs, the reference is to *der Mensch,* or "mankind." The narrative gesture behind such a moment is one that includes us in the process of the particular affliction being described; in this sense, all of us are implicated in the condition—which is not dependent on clinical illness—of knowing of death before it comes to us. And for that condition, one of metaphysical questioning, there is no known antidote.

Much of the power of this moment of inwardness in the novel (as of so many others) derives from the fact that the metaphysical argument is so firmly grounded in particular, realistically perceived contexts. Hanno's rejection of the call of life derives from a medically realistic—that is, clinical—description of the course of a disease. When Hanno makes his rapturous music, he does so in the suitably grand surroundings of his parental home and after a ghastly day at school. Thomas's philosophical reverie does not exempt him from carrying on with his life as a merchant and senator. It cannot be emphasized too strongly that the interludes of intense inwardness that have concerned us in this chapter have not in any sense transcended or canceled out the realistic mode, that precise acknowledgment of social facts and circumstances which continues to form the basis of the novel's style and theme. Even Hanno's supreme moment of life-or-death choice is scrupulously prepared for, as we have seen, through scenes, images, and arguments in the realistic mode. Much the same holds true for all the death scenes in the novel. For instance, in the death of Elisabeth, Thomas's mother, the medical symptoms are accurately rendered. So too is the psychological argument: Elisabeth fights death every inch of the way because she has always been unequivocally and joyously anchored in life. Unlike Hanno, she has not known misery or pain before the onset of her final illness. Hence, she makes no concessions—until they are forced from her. The narrator modulates into the first person plural pronoun whereby we as readers are asked to assent to the truth of psychologically intelligible processes:

> This sickness, this infection of the lungs has forced its way into her upright body without any preparatory psychological work having occurred that might have made the destruction easier . . . that undermining process of suffering which gradually removes us through pain from life itself, or at least from the conditions under which we have received it, and which awakens in us the sweet longing for an end, for other conditions, or for peace. (IX, 1, 440)

We note the generality injected into the passage by the use of the pronoun "we" and by the present tense. A similar effect is achieved in the description of Hanno's death from typhoid whereby Hanno becomes "der Mensch," or humankind. Yet we also note the lacerating clinical realism of both death scenes, and the fact that both passages draw on the psychology of illness for their truthfulness. The philosophical-cum-metaphysical issue is part of a richly detailed and explored account of everyday life and behavior. Here too inward matters are inseparable from outward matters.

Buddenbrooks begins and ends with the declaration of one particular form of inwardness—religious faith. It opens with Tony's recitation of an article from the catechism, and it ends with Sesemi Weichbrodt's triumphant assertion of faith in an afterlife.[6] Thus the alpha and omega of the novel have to do with matters not of the psyche but of the soul. Yet clearly we do not understand *Buddenbrooks* as a religious novel but as predominantly one of family life, and the changes that mark the sequence of generations whose fortunes we follow are symptomatic of changes in the society at large. The inwardness of the novel has to do with Mann's perception that religious, spiritual, or metaphysical experiences are implicated in public, outward concerns, in the precise sense that the corporate cohesion of any society is so often constituted by shared inwardness, by agreement as to the validity of certain ideas, concepts, and terms such that they become second nature. As successive generations of Buddenbrooks find it increasingly difficult to acknowledge the corporate assumptions of their culture, they come to notice and to reflect on them. In so doing, even in the privacy of the thoughts they share with no one, they debate with and within the terms of experience as made available, articulate, and comprehensible in the discourse of their society.

The invocation of religious faith at both the beginning and end of the novel has, then, a great deal to do with inwardness as comprehended in social (that is, realistic) terms. We are concerned less with theology as the definition of a transcendent realm than with theology as part of a matrix of values by which a society works.[7] We are close to the kind of understanding that Max Weber and R. H. Tawney expressed in their two famous studies[8] of the extent to which and the ways in which religious belief can be profoundly constitutive of socio-economic behavior. As so often happens, the work of sociologists, historians, and political theoreticians confirms what has been perceived before them by creative writers. As Mann commented in the *Reflections of an Unpolitical Man,*

Inwardness

> I set some store by the notion that I sensed and came up with the thought that the modern capitalist, competitive type, the bourgeois with his *ascetic* idea of professional duty is a product of a Protestant ethic, of Puritanism and Calvinism—and I did so off my own bat, with no prior reading, as a pure perception of my own. Only afterwards . . . did I notice that the thought was at the same time being thought and expressed by scholarly thinkers.[9]

As both a corroboration and an extension of these issues having to do with historicized inwardness, music also plays a role of particular importance in the novel, and it demands consideration in its own right.

10

Music

Readers often have the impression that music enters the consciousness and sensibility of the Buddenbrook family only with Gerda and Hanno. To all intents and purposes this is true, but even in regard to this theme part I prefigures what is to come. After dinner, the group of men splits up: some stay with the women, but the others go with Jean on a tour of inspection of the newly acquired house, ending with coffee and cigars in the billiard room. Those who stay behind hear old Johann playing the flute, accompanied by his daughter-in-law:

> The six gentlemen could still hear as they walked through the pil-
> lared hall the first notes on the flute, accompanied by the Konsulin
> on the harmonium, filling the "landscape room," a modest, clear,
> thoughtful melody that hovered eloquently through the expanse of
> rooms. The Consul listened as long as the music could be heard. He
> would have been all too willing to stay behind in the "landscape
> room," to sit in an armchair and, surrounded by these notes, to
> indulge his dreams and feelings; but duties of hospitality. . . . (I, 8,
> 26–27)

The key point here is that music is associated with Jean's dreams and emotions, with that inwardness and religious feeling that comes increasingly into conflict with his duties as a Buddenbrook. In terms of the appeal it holds for Jean, music implies a departure from the integral and secure way of life the house provides.

Two central matters, one philosophical and the other historical, that inform the whole understanding of music in *Buddenbrooks*, appear in chapter 6 of part VIII. Insofar as the nature and being of music is explored, Mann is clearly indebted to Schopenhauer. In his philosophy, Schopenhauer accorded a particular status to art and the artist because they stood for a mode of will-less contemplation of the savage turmoil of life. Art, so his argument runs, offers an image of the World-as-Will, but because that image is, precisely, an aesthetic picturing of the world and not the unmediated world itself, the Will in all its fury is held at bay. But Schopenhauer, in a most extraordinary piece of paradoxical but wonderfully illuminating reasoning, sees fit to describe music as the highest of the arts because it alone offers the very substance of the Will. The paradox resides in the fact that one would expect Schopenhauer, on his own terms, to accord music supreme status among the arts because it is the most abstract, the least referential and earthbound.

Music does not copy the shapes and textures of the Will's self-realization in the palpable world; music does not mean anything precise or verifiable. A C major chord may feel uplifting, triumphant, affirmatory, or whatever, but in and of itself it does not refer to any experience. But surprisingly, it is not this aspect of music, not its being pure form without substantial content, that Schopenhauer singles out for praise. Quite the reverse. He perceives that music, precisely by virtue of being nonspecific, nonparticular, can operate simply at the level of patterned expectation and fulfillment and thereby speaks directly to the flux and sway of human emotions. In this sense, music gives us not the causes and occasions of human feeling, but the very buildup and release, the ebb and flow, of primal emotional patterns. The paradox is striking because one would expect Schopenhauer to reject as unaesthetic any art that offers the Will in unfiltered expression. But what Schopenhauer's philosophy and aesthetics may lose in conceptual rigor they gain enormously in suggestiveness and resonance. Surely Schopenhauer's paradox is, in a sense, the paradox of music itself: will-less, sublime, disembodied mathematical patterns on the one hand; pure pulse, drive, energy, untrammeled Will on the other.

This rich central perception can be discerned in the two descriptions we are given of Hanno's music. The little piece he plays on the evening of his eighth birthday has a conclusion that he loves dearly (despite the disapproval of Herr Pfühl, the local organist and his music teacher). That conclusion is described as one that "in primitive elevation placed the crown on the whole piece" (VIII, 6, 398). The paradox of primitivism and elevation ("primitive Gehobenheit") is related to that which Schopenhauer discerned in music. And it is also invoked when Hanno's last improvisation at the piano is described: "There was something brutal and coarse, and at the same time something ascetic and religious, something akin to belief and self-sacrifice, in the fanatical cult of this nothing, this scrap of melody, this short, childish, harmonic invention of one and a half bars" (XI, 2, 588). Even Hanno's music, which, from the impassioned description given of it, is all about the Will as orgiastic tumult, apparently also partakes of the paradox we have been discussing: the sexual climax in which the music culminates also speaks of negation of the will, of spirituality and transcendence. It is significant that the same rhetorical phrases indicating the coming of revelation are common both to Thomas's Schopenhauer moment and to Hanno's music:

> And behold: suddenly it was as though the darkness were rent asunder before his eyes, as though the velvet wall of night split wide open. (X, 5, 512)

> And he lay still and waited fervently, and felt himself tempted to pray that it might come again and illuminate him. And it came. (512)

> And behold, suddenly there was, in sound colours of matt silver, the first motif again. (XI, 2, 586)

> And it came, it could be withheld no longer, the spasms of longing could be no longer prolonged, it came, just as when a curtain parts,

gates are opened, thorn hedges separate and walls of fire suddenly
sink into nothingness. (587)

The rhetoric of sudden knowing and seeing, of blissful, overwhelming
illumination is common to those moments of inwardness in the novel
that promise release, elation, and even triumph—to Thomas's reading
of philosophy, to Hanno's music. The "behold" and the "and it came"
are the stylistic signatures of those rapturous moments, those epiphan-
ies that take Thomas and Hanno beyond the parameters and obligations of their daily lives. Both father and son, in the moments of their
most profound self-exploration, find themselves in paradoxical realms
in which the acknowledgment of the life force coexists with the need
to negate, indeed to transcend, it. In such moments we register the
ways in which both figures find in the promptings of their own hearts
and minds some of the deepest philosophical disturbances of their age.

As with so many of the moments of philosophical inwardness, so
too with music the metaphysical issue interlocks with the realistic (and
historical) argument. In regard to the music described, Mann is at
pains to highlight considerations of cultural specificity. A good example of this is seen in chapter 6 of part VIII with the introduction of
Herr Pfühl, who makes music with Gerda and teaches Hanno harmony and counterpoint. Herr Pfühl, a church organist, has written,
we gather, a small book on the keys of sacred music and is a great
lover of the music of J. S. Bach. Although he is prepared to concede
that Bach's harmonic skill may have initiated developments that issue
in the (to Herr Pfühl) barbaric practices of contemporary music, he
insists that the true glory of Bach's achievement is to be found in the
splendid architecture of its counterpoint. Some of Bach's spirit, indeed,
is to be heard in Herr Pfühl's own compositions:

> These compositions and the fantasies and variations he performed
> on Sundays in St. Mary's Church were unassailable, immaculate,
> filled with the irresistible, imposing, moral and logical dignity of
> the Strict Form. The essence of such music was foreign to all earthly
> beauty, and what it expressed did not speak to the human feelings

of any lay person. What spoke out of them and what dominated in them was technique that had become an ascetic religion, was skill raised to the level of an end in itself, of absolute sanctity. (VIII, 6, 390–91)

Herr Pfühl is a fierce opponent of modern music. He is outraged when Gerda first asks him to play from the piano score of Wagner's *Tristan und Isolde,* dismissing the score as "demagogy, blasphemy, and madness . . . the end of all morality in art" (VIII, 6, 392). But Gerda manages to persuade him to play at least certain pages from Wagner. And at one point he even plays Wagner of his own accord:

> While Gerda, with her violin under her arm, was looking for some music, something extraordinary happened: Herr Pfühl, Edmund Pfühl, organist at the Church of St. Mary, gradually moved in his improvisation into a very strange style, and as he did so, a kind of shameful happiness shone in the distant gaze of his eyes. . . . Beneath his fingers there began a swelling and blossoming, an interweaving and singing, out of which quietly at first and fading again, then more clear and muscular in its statement, in its skilled counterpoint, an old-fashionedly grandiose, wondrously ceremonial march motif emerged. . . . A climax, a retreat, a transition . . . and with the resolution the violin entered fortissimo. The *Meistersinger* Prelude unfolded. (392)

We are told that *Die Meistersinger* is the Wagner opera with which Herr Pfühl can most readily come to terms. The description of the Prelude suggests why; Wagner's score does indeed consciously look back to older forms of music, to chorales, to modes of early church music, yet it marries them to the harmonic sophistication of modern chromaticism. That characteristic sense of the immense harmonic power of Wagner, of textures of swelling and fading, of blissfully and chromatically prolonged postponements, of full-throated thematic statement is rendered very powerfully in the narrative description of the *Meistersinger* Prelude.

As Herr Pfühl plays, Gerda's violin enters just after the transition and resolution *(Auflösung).* That, both as a technical term for a resolution in music and as a term expressing disorder and dissolution, is, as we have noted, central to Hanno's music and to the illness that destroys him.

At the end of chapter 6 we are given a description of Hanno's birthday concert, at which he and his mother perform one of his compositions. It is a piece that depends on a "little melodic invention that was of more harmonic than rhythmic character" (VIII, 6, 398). At the climax of the piece, the restatement of this little phrase is held at bay, delayed by dissonances:

> He denied himself the resolution, he kept it from himself and his hearers. What would it be, this resolution, this blissful and liberated descent into B Major? . . . Not yet, not yet. One further moment of postponement, of delay, of suspense that had to become unbearable in order that the fulfillment should be more delicious. . . . One last, final tasting of this pulsing and thrusting longing, of this craving of the whole will. . . . It came, came over him, and he no longer resisted. (VIII, 6, 398–99)

Here we have a vivid expression of a particular kind of music. At one level, we hear the argument, reminiscent of Schopenhauer's perception of music as the Will itself, that music consists essentially of patterns of expectation and fulfillment. The ear knows that the climax of Hanno's music will be the restatement of the first subject. The hammering dissonances that obstruct the resolution serve to intensify the longing and expectation and to make the final attainment of the key and the restatement of the first subject the more overwhelming in their sense of homecoming achieved, of a triumphant return to first, indeed to primal, things. Hanno's music clearly speaks—and in the narrator's account is made quite explicitly to speak—of orgiastic emotions that issue from bedrock levels of feeling and being. At the same time that we register this Schopenhauerian perception, however, we also register that this is a particular kind of music, music with a historical signature to it. This is not music in the spirit of Bach, Haydn, or Mozart; it is Wagnerian in its feeling, texture, and argument.

When, during his moment of intense illumination as he reads the book of philosophy, Thomas Buddenbrook comes to think and reflect, he does so within the philosophic modes and concepts that are part of the cultural temper of his age. Similarly, when Hanno makes music, it is recognizably the music of his age and his culture: it is Wagnerian chromaticism that we are confronted with.[1] The philosophical argument about the nature of music itself coexists with the historical argument about the change in musical language from the essentially contrapuntal (Bach) to the essentially (and chromatically) harmonic (Wagner).

When, in part I, Jean wishes he could stay in the "landscape room" and listen to his father's flute, it is, of course, a very different kind of music that he would have heard. Old Johann, we know, is very much a man of the eighteenth century. He plays the flute.[2] The details perhaps coalesce to suggest that *that* music, in the spirit of Frederick the Great and his love for the flute, would have been classical, balanced, formally contained. It would have expressed the correlative in moral and social terms of the music's own formal and aesthetic character; it would have validated a balanced, controlled, ordered life. The music of Hanno's age is very different; its aesthetic forms express passion and volatility. Hence, the music of which Hanno is capable links him, even in his radical repudiation of the social values all around him, with that society. Even something as abstract and as emotionally self-absorbed as Hanno's improvisations are part of the public discourse of the age. To that discourse in its socioeconomic aspects I want now to turn.

11

Of Economic
Signs and Symbols

Alongside its concern with the modes in which inwardness is expressed in each Buddenbrook generation, Thomas Mann's novel also maintains a consistent interest in the changing climate of economic life in the social and business world. This is a strand that begins at the opening of the novel, in 1835, merely one year after the organization of the Zollverein. By dismantling some of the many tariff and currency barriers among the various principalities and states of the German Confederation, the Zollverein gradually started the movement toward the establishment of German unity under Prussian leadership in 1871. The Zollverein is discussed after dinner at the new Buddenbrook house in the Mengstrasse. Jean is very much in favor because he feels it will invigorate the economy: "In the Zollverein Mecklenburg and Schleswig-Holstein would be open to us" (I, 8, 29). But there is no shortage of dissenting voices to regret the surrender of sovereignty that would be entailed:

> "And our autonomy? And our independence? . . . What about them? Would Hamburg be prepared to go along with this Prussian invention? Do we want to be swallowed up immediately, Budden-

brook? God preserve us, no: what use is the Zollverein to us, I should like to know? Isn't all going well as it is?" (I, 8, 28–29)

Jean can deal with the last question without difficulty; all is not going well economically with the free city of Lübeck. But even he is prepared to mourn the loss of local autonomy that would be entailed and to concede the value of a system in which the civic authority is prepared to stand surety for a financial undertaking given on a citizen's oath. But Senator Langhals thinks otherwise:

> "Of course I am no merchant . . . but if I am to be honest,—no, that whole business with the citizen's oath is gradually becoming a nonsense—that's what I would have to say! It has become a formality that is taken lightly . . . and the state suffers in the process."
> (29)

The discussion of the Zollverein is interrupted by the entrance of Herr Hoffstede, the genial town poet, and there the subject is left.

This conversation, handled, like so much else in the exposition, with great casualness, inaugurates a series of socioeconomic arguments that will run through the novel. What is at stake is not so much a detailed fictional re-creation involving precise figures, statistics of specific economic indicators and tendencies; rather, Thomas Mann captures with wonderful thoughtfulness the point at which economic processes interlock with psychological ones. In the course of the novel we are given figures about the Buddenbrook fortune, but these figures merely provide a sense of plausible detail, of Henry James's notion of "solidity of specification."[1] What counts for the purposes of this novel is the Buddenbrooks' sense of their own wealth (or lack of it), their perception of how that wealth is or should be earned, how solid it is, and so on. The discussion of the Zollverein has the allusive richness of so much of the novel's realism; the new trend is felt as a crisis of values, as a sociopsychological disturbance. The Zollverein is perceived as a threat to a particular form of socioeconomic organization, one that is characterized by familial intimacy and by a quasi-feudal, guild-based economy. It was only in 1866 that Lübeck started to dismantle the monopoly of the guilds. Lindtke in his study *Die Stadt der Buddenbrooks* highlights the many ways in which nineteenth-century Lübeck resisted patterns of economic and social change; in 1831 the town had 24,000 inhabitants, and in 1867 30,500, whereas over the same period Hamburg and Bremen had roughly doubled in size. Lübeck was the last town in Germany to give up locking its city gates, and it did so only in 1864. A guidebook for 1866 describes the dominant impression made by its architecture as "a colossal piece of the Middle Ages which previous centuries have left unscathed and which thrusts its way intact and defiant into the modern world."[2] The threat to local autonomy, to the civic protectionism of this small Free City posed by the demands of a modern, efficient economy was one that called into question a whole way of life, a complex fabric of conventions, assumptions, and values. It is this disturbance that Mann illuminates in his novel.

The principal rivals of the Buddenbrooks are the Hagenströms. They have not been living long in Lübeck, and they are, in consequence, regarded as upstarts. Hinrich Hagenström and his son Hermann display both ambition and considerable business acumen. Moreover, both of them are clearly interested in establishing themselves socially and administratively within the town.

Some years after he had finished writing *Buddenbrooks*, Thomas Mann commented that he himself had never been particularly aware of or interested in socioeconomic developments, that he had slept through them. But the novel knew better than did its maker and registered the seismic shifts via the subliminal cognition of artistic creation: "The problem that I was itching to deal with, and that made me productive, was not a political one but a biological, psychological one; . . . the human and spiritual issues concerned me—I only semiconsciously picked up the sociological and political dimension, it concerned me little."[3]

Just before the outbreak of World War I, Werner Sombart wrote *Der Bourgeois: Zur Geistesgeschichte des modernen Wirtschaftsmenschen* in which he made a crucial distinction between the old-fashioned, static, patriarchally minded "Bürger" and the modern, quick-witted, speculatively entrepreneurial "Bourgeois." Sombart's case study is, one suspects, very much indebted to Thomas Mann's novel. Since its appearance, much ink has been spilt over the question whether the Buddenbrooks and the Hagenströms do, in fact, adequately represent two radically divergent forms of economic activity.[4] It has been pointed out that the Hagenströms are too similar to the Buddenbrooks to represent their diametrical opposites. They buy the old Buddenbrook house in the Mengstrasse, so presumably they are not indifferent to the old emblems, to mottoes such as "Dominus providebit" over the door. Certainly, Moritz Hagenström, the brother of Hermann, shows signs of Buddenbrook-like weakness and sensitivity. Perhaps it would be more accurate to say that, just as the Buddenbrooks succeed the Ratenkamps after they have gone into decline, so too the Hagenströms will succeed the Buddenbrooks, only to be supplanted in their turn. Moreover, much of what we know of the Hagenströms is filtered through the Buddenbrook consciousness. The novel does not provide a simple allegorical juxtaposition of the Buddenbrooks as traditional, patriarchal *Bürger* on the one hand and the Hagenströms as ruthless capitalists on the other. The one-to-one equivalence simply does not work, and Mann recognized as much in his *Reflections of an Unpolitical Man:*

> I never portrayed [the type of the new 'Bürger'] as a real, as a political and economic phenomenon; neither my sympathy nor my knowledge extended to this. But the poetic dimension always seemed to me to be the symbolic one, and I can say that I have written almost nothing that was not symbolic of the heroism of this modern, unbourgeois kind. Indeed, seen in this light, Thomas Buddenbrook is not only a German "Bürger" but also a modern "Bourgeois."[5]

The real import of the Hagenströms in regard to the sociological argument of the novel lies not in any outward, allegorical behavior on their part but in their being a crucial part of the sociopsychological consciousness of the Buddenbrooks. The inner crises that afflict the later Buddenbrooks express their sense of the profound sea change that is occurring all around them in terms of social, economic, and mercantile values.[6] In one sense, the change is happening primarily inside them. But it is no less real on that account, and the inwardness that the novel charts so magnificently is no less revealing for that. The gulf between the Buddenbrooks and the Hagenströms is *felt* by the Buddenbrooks to be unbridgeable. The symbolic patterns of the novel express not so much palpable facts as the felt, value-heavy symbolizations of social life.

Chapter 1 of part IV gives the text of a letter that Jean writes to Thomas; he invokes the family motto "My son, be with pleasure about thy business by day, but only make such business that we may sleep peacefully at night." He then goes on to express what he perceives as the gulf between that ethos of religiously moderated business enterprise and the fierce competitiveness of the Hagenströms: "I intend to keep this principle sacred to my life's end, although sometimes one has one's doubts at the sight of people who do better without such principles. I am thinking of Strunck and Hagenström who are manifestly expanding, while our affairs are proceeding at all too quiet a pace" (IV, 1, 137).

That contrast is repeated a generation later in the rivalry between Thomas Buddenbrook and Hermann Hagenström for the vacant seat on the Senate. The narrator summarizes what is clearly the townspeople's perception of the symbolic contrast between the two men:

> The casual and generous way in which he [Hermann Hagenström] earned and spent money was very different from the tenacious, patient work, sternly guided by inherited principles, of his fellow merchants. This man stood free of the hindering fetters of traditional piety on his own two feet, and everything old-fashioned was foreign to him. . . . He was not the man to vote in the city council for the granting of large sums of money for the restoration and preservation of medieval monuments. But that he was the first, absolutely the first in the whole town to light his living quarters and his offices with gas, that was a fact. . . .
> The prestige of Thomas Buddenbrook was of a different kind. He

was not only himself; people respected in him the still unforgotten personalities of his father, grandfather, and great-grandfather. (VII, 3, 321)

Occasional subtle hints, such as the emphasis on Hermann Hagenström's being the first to light with gas ("that was a fact"), help us to realize that what we are reading is not so much an authoritative, narratorial comparison of the two men as a paraphrase of the citizens' perceptions of these two figures—and of these perceptions as symbolizing deeply felt patterns of socioeconomic change.

Thomas Buddenbrook's career is, of course, not without its business successes. Before the stages of decline set in, there are moments when he rejoices in his own dynamism, in his ability to be party to the new trends in the business world:

> Soon it was noteworthy that, since Thomas Buddenbrook had held the reins in his hands, a more inspired, fresher, and more enterprising spirit prevailed in the business. Here and there something was risked, here and there the credit of the house, which under the earlier regime had been merely an idea, a theory, a luxury, was deployed and used with self-confidence. . . . The gentlemen at the stock exchange nodded to each other. "Buddenbrook wants to make his money work for him," they said. (V, 3, 208–9)

Here we get a glimpse of a Buddenbrook who delights in the insubstantiality (by earlier standards) of modern money making. The key factors in the modern game are intangibles having to do with "good name," with credit generating credit, with money making money. Thomas also delights in his own skills, his charm as a businessman, almost as though the process of risking his own neck is part of the excitement of operating within the new market. He says at one point:

> A businessman should not be a bureaucrat! . . . Personality is involved—and that is my style. . . . I constantly feel the need to have an immediate impact on the course of things by virtue of a glance, a word, a gesture . . . to control matters by the immediate influence

of my will, my talent, my luck—or however you want to call it. (V, 3, 209)

This is the exultation of someone who rejoices in the very volatility of the processes he can manipulate. Luck breeds luck. Charm breeds success, and no other, more visible, means of support seems to be necessary.

Yet increasingly, as the novel unfolds, Thomas becomes less sure of himself, more inward-looking, more troubled and thoughtful. The Pöppenrade harvest brings matters to a head, as we have already seen. When Tony first mentions the possibility, Thomas instantly answers her in the spirit of the family motto that allows only such business to be done as is consonant with a good night's sleep afterward. But once he is left alone, the agony begins. The sense of the brutality of life, represented in its most unadorned form by the business world, haunts Thomas as an offense against all decent human feeling. Yet, just as he has done before, so this time too he persuades himself to serve the brutality that disgusts him—to go in for the high-risk deal. One of the arguments he invokes to quell his eroding self-doubts is that this particular deal, while savoring of a typical Hagenström "coup," actually needs the personal touch, the subtle and complex style of a Buddenbrook:

> No, Messrs. Strunck and Hagenström would not be able to land this catch! . . . Indeed, the personal touch was decisive here. It was no ordinary transaction that one could handle coolly and within the usual forms. Rather, given Tony's mediation, it had the character of a private matter, which was to be handled with discretion and tact. Ah, no, Hermann Hagenström was scarcely the man for this deal! (VIII, 4, 374)

The psychological turmoil Thomas experiences generates a series of philosophical questions that derive from and feed into a consideration of questions of economic behavior and market probity. The moment of inwardness involves a spectrum of concerns extending from the metaphysical to the mundane. Jochen Vogt, among other critics, has suggested that the Pöppenrade harvest deal is not an adequate representation of the emergence of a new, speculative economy, because the risk is anchored in natural forces and not in the rapid movements of the money markets.[7] Factually this is true. But Thomas, as he agonizes, has no doubt as to the symbolic value of the harvest deal. And once he invests the deal with this kind of significance, then the risk to him, to his sense of values, to his way of life, is real.

Moreover, the sense of an inevitable change with respect to moral and business values is a constant facet of Thomas's experience. Herr Weinschenk, the husband of his niece Erika, is arrested and subsequently convicted for a piece of sharp business practice that, however, is more often than not accepted without demur. Thomas tries to explain matters to his mother:

> There is in modern business practice a thing called "usance". . . . "Usance," you see, is a maneuver that is not entirely above reproach, that is not fully to be reconciled with the letter of the law and that to the layperson looks pretty dishonest, but yet, according to unspoken agreements within the business world, it is absolutely common practice. . . . If Weinschenk has offended, he has probably not behaved any worse than many of his colleagues who have got away with it entirely. (VIII, 8, 413)

We hear Thomas's profound unease in this speech, an unease that has to do with his sense that the worlds of money and business efficiency have moved rapidly into certain kinds of behavior that are offensive to established moral and legal codes.[8] In just the same way, his first reaction to the Pöppenrade deal is to question its probity and decency, while at the same time feeling that it is the kind of thing that modern business practice acknowledges as perfectly acceptable. Every time this kind of crisis befalls Thomas he is weakened, weakened because the crisis convinces him that, despite all his efforts, a gulf has opened up between his most profound convictions and values and what he perceives as the prevailing socioeconomic trends. He consequently feels himself increasingly out of touch with what he tells himself is a rapidly changing world.

Thomas is not, we must remember, a simple reactionary in terms of economic and business acumen. Like his father, he is in favor of the Zollverein, as he explains to Herr Wenzel, his barber, in chapter 7 of part VI. He even recalls for us (lest we had forgotten) the presence of Hoffstede the poet at a discussion of the same issue many years earlier. The reference, of course, is to the conversation in part I. Thomas Buddenbrook is in favor of improvements to the postal service that have come about by amalgamating small firms of carriers, and of the replacement of oil lamps by gas lamps. In all kinds of ways, then, he is not opposed to modern developments. Yet in so much of his everyday work he constantly finds the unreality, the insubstantiality of modern business practice an offense to his preference for solidity in human, social, and economic affairs. When he is trying to resist Tony's advocacy of the Pöppenrade deal, he speaks of his proven ability to deal with minor landed gentry who regard merchants—in this case, buyers, shippers, and exporters of grain—as faintly disreputable because they are parasitic on the labor of the true wealth creators:

> You know there is among them [the gentry] one or the other who does not accord merchants a great deal of respect, although they are as necessary to him as he is to them, who tends to overemphasize the (up to a point undeniable) superiority of the producer over the middleman in business affairs—and to see the merchant as little better than the Jewish peddler whom one allows to have one's old clothes with the distinct feeling of being outmaneuvered. I flatter myself that in general I have not made the impression of a morally questionable trickster on these gentlemen. (VIII, 2, 439)

Thomas's little pen portrait of a particular social class is tinged with an admixture of envy. Up to a point, he believes that they are right to have infinitely less respect for marketing, for buying and selling, for middlemen than for genuine agrarian productivity. He is proud of his ability to have them accept him as one of them. But he feels that the business world is moving remorselessly even farther away from the substantiality of productivity into the abstractions of marketing and selling.

Thomas's sense of solidity versus insubstantiality is expressed nowhere more poignantly than in the words he speaks about the grandiose new house in the Fischergrube. Its completion coincides with his sense that success is beginning to desert him. Success, he reflects bitterly, is less a matter of facts than of feelings, and the requisite feelings are no longer his:

> What is success? . . . The awareness that alone by virtue of my presence I can exert pressure on the movements of life all around me. . . . Luck and success are in us. We must hold on to them, firmly, profoundly. As soon as here inside us something begins to weaken, to grow slack and tired, then everything comes loose all around us, rebels, withdraws from our influence. (VII, 6, 337f.)

Like Arthur Miller's Willy Loman in *Death of a Salesman,* Thomas Buddenbrook senses that his life is being hollowed out by the insubstantiality of the trader's existence.

Psychological and economic concerns constantly interact in *Buddenbrooks,* and it is in this nexus that the Buddenbrooks' experiences are shown to reflect tendencies on their society. I must caution here, however, that attempts to establish one-to-one equivalences between events in the lives of Mann's fictional family and trends in nineteenth-century Germany tend to endow various episodes with greater allegorical loads than they can carry. If we are to consider how fictional life can reflect sociological and historical truths, we must keep distinct the definitions of "average" and "typical." The story of the Buddenbrook decline is by no means one of everyday events in the lives of average people of the time. The Buddenbrooks, in the exceptional and radical nature of what they experience, typify in heightened form gradual and diffuse changes in society, and it is above all the inwardness of these changes—these shifts in values, in the complex texture of assumptions, conventions, and principles—that the novel registers.

Of Economic Signs and Symbols

The Mengstrasse house embodies just such a way of life: it enshrines the ethos sometimes referred to as "das ganze Haus," "the whole house."[10] The house is not only a residential building, a family home, but also a place of business. Carts loaded with grain go through the great central entrance into a yard and warehouse area at the back; the firm's administrative offices are in the house itself. In visible terms the house expresses the unity of family and firm; the wealth and position of the Buddenbrooks is palpably present in the sacks of grain constantly going in and out. Business correspondence, ledgers, and money are not divorced from the physical commodities traded; the realm of mercantile existence is literally under the same roof as the family's domestic quarters. The new house Thomas has built in the Fischergrube is more grandiose, but it is emblematic of a fragmented, abstract, and isolated way of life. The transition from one house to the other—from a quasi-feudal order to a more modern, capitalist way of life—is central to Mann's story and to the typicality of the Buddenbrooks' decline. The shift in values expresses a complex of socioeconomic developments.

The Mengstrasse house typifies the traditional character and way of life of the town in which the novel is set. The Buddenbrook ethos partakes of what Mack Walker has defined as the symbolic nexus of the German "hometowns." Though urban in character—with artisans and tradespeople, a developed civic administration, and strong commodity and trading markets—these hometowns were self-contained and defiantly inward-looking. They continued to be sustained by a guild ethos and were often dominated by key dynastic families. As the German-speaking lands moved toward unification under Prussian rule in the last part of the nineteenth century, the hometown ethos was doomed as the operative market became a national—indeed, an international—one.

This process comes up in the conversation about the Zollverein in part I of *Buddenbrooks*. Progressives advocate the Customs Union; conservatives regret the demise of local autonomy and communal intimacy. Richard Wagner's great operatic tribute to the hometowns, *Die Meistersinger,* was written in 1868, the same year Lübeck joined the Zollverein. We will recall that the Prelude to *Die Meistersinger* is the one piece of modern music that comes nearest to finding favor with Herr Pfühl, who in general resents the harmonic slipperiness of contemporary musical idiom but can cherish this work because it is anchored in the more dependable (social and musical) forms of an earlier age. I am not, however, pointing up one-to-one equivalences here. As a Free City and a constituent member of the Hanseatic League, Lübeck does not, strictly speaking, qualify as one of Walker's hometowns. Moreover, both Jean and Thomas Buddenbrook are in favor of the Zollverein, whereas, if they were straightforward allegories of the traditional, and hence threatened, order, they would be staunch supporters of local autonomy. The quality and the inner character of the change chronicled in *Buddenbrooks* has to do with the "decline" not just of one family but of a whole way of life, many of whose features Walker has identified.

It is extraordinary that *Buddenbrooks* nowhere identifies by name the town that is its setting. Generations of readers have known that town to be Lübeck: so many of the topographical facts, right down to the street names, tally. It is almost as though Mann did not need to name Lübeck in his novel because it was simply too familiar to him and to others who knew the town. The setting for this novel is a town that is a mentality, a corpus of intellectual, moral, and economic assumptions. In a lecture Mann delivered in his hometown, published as the essay "Lübeck as a Form of Mental and Spiritual Life," he quoted from *Reflections of an Unpolitical Man*, written some years before:

> I am a town dweller, a citizen [Bürger], a child and great-grandchild of German bourgeois [bürgerlich] culture. . . . Were my forefathers not artisans from Nuremberg of that type which Germany exported throughout the world and even to the Far East, as a proof that it was the country of towns? They sat as town councilors in Mecklenburg, they came to Lübeck, they were merchants of the Holy Roman Empire—and by writing the story of their house, a *civic* chronicle modulated into a naturalistic novel, . . . I proved to be much less removed from their way of life than I allowed myself to imagine.[11]

Similarly in the Lübeck essay, he expresses his profound attachment to the town, to "Lübeck as a town, as the shape and character of a town." The German phrase thrice repeats the noun *Stadt:* "Lübeck als Stadt, als Stadtbild und Stadtcharakter." And Mann goes on to invoke the particular intensity of its urban existence: "It is an urban, a town identity that it has, if one is to capture its essence in one concept. And one could say that the landscape of a town is its architecture, Lübeck Gothic in our case."[12] We might say, then, that Lübeck is not allegorically symptomatic but symbolically representative of a particular ethos central to the German lands before 1871.

Buddenbrooks begins in that loose aggregation of states, territories, and principalities that was the legacy of the Holy Roman Empire to the German-speaking lands in the nineteenth century. It concludes—four years after the establishment of Wilhelmine Germany—in a unified nation-state that by the turn of the century will have become a formidable industrial and economic power. In terms of its foreground events—of explicit discussions or detailed portrayal of political circumstances—the novel has next to nothing to say about this momentous transformation in the life of a nation. Yet it charts, as does no other fictional work known to me, the shift in values that that transformation entailed. The hometown's hold on the corporate imagination of the inhabitants of German lands, whether hometown dwellers or not, was and is prodigious. The change wrought by the unification of 1871 was astonishing in terms of its precipitate in the inner life of the individual German. And *Buddenbrooks* captures this change through that mode which is so much more appropriate to the imaginative writer than to the social or economic historian—symbolic statement. Symbolic statement is capable of capturing socioeconomic matters at the exact point where forms of socioeconomic behavior are particularly informed by symbolic signification. For example, notions of a traditional community and way of life, and of changes affecting the traditional, inherited value scales, are examples of where extraliterary behavior constantly generates symbols in order to express the felt life within. The novelist does not need to invent these symbols; the social world provides them in abundance. The novelist may need only to eavesdrop—and to orchestrate and shape these symbols.

Buddenbrooks ultimately works through the patterns and textures of symbolic organization and, by so doing, captures with great precision and eloquence the processes of familial and social change. The Buddenbrooks are a dynastic family; they are submerged in the recurring rituals, in the symbolic occasions and sacramental customs that make up their dynastic way of living. In the early stages of the novel, the characters tend to live within the symbolic modes of Buddenbrook existence without particularly reflecting on them or even being aware of them. Those symbols are, we might say, second nature. The successive generations become more inwardly questioning and more reflective as the novel progresses, and then they begin to notice the symbols. They do so precisely because these symbols have become problematic, either in the sense of being so much dead weight or in that they have become weightless because their indwelling meaning has fled.

The novel opens with notions of symbols that are theologically underwritten; Tony recites her catechism, Jean entrusts his ecstatic outpourings of faith to the family chronicle. Both subscribe with a minimum of questioning to the symbols of Buddenbrook existence and the sacraments of that faith according to which the Lord does indeed provide for the Buddenbrooks. But Thomas's uncertainty is subversive of any such certainty, and his sense of desubstantialized or despiritualized symbols feeds into the changes in economic and business life that so perturb him. As the ethos of modern business practice moves away from dealing in commodities to dealing in money, so there is a shift from outward and visible wealth (a sack of grain) to the merely notional entity of the unit of currency. Money is a currency of tokens and signs; if money can be made without reference to commodities, then tokens acquire a certain substantiality because commodities have been rendered insubstantial.

The Buddenbrooks realize that it is the Hagenströms and not they who are highly capable of dealing with—and in—the alarmingly volatile markets where the value of a commodity is anchored not in its inherent quality but in its exchange value, in that mechanism which renders it infinitely negotiable by constantly converting it into what it is not. The Hagenströms speculate in money; the later Buddenbrooks speculate with ideas generated by their own sense of rootlessness. Common to both is the process of dealing consciously with symbols whose values shift constantly. Once again we find that it is at the symbolic level that psychological and economic issues interact; symbols, like currencies, can be brought into circulation and then withdrawn. The economy of the marketplace is one of signs that impinges on the economy of the Buddenbrook psyche. Their seemingly private dilemmas, constantly enacted as they are in terms of (and in consciousness of) the symbols by which they feel themselves required to live, register profound disturbances in the corporate world.[13]

12

The Family and Its Symbols

Because of the intense symbolism of Buddenbrook living, the symbolic mode is a property of both the experiences chronicled in the novel and the novel that does the chronicling.[1] Thomas Mann does not stylize the family for his aesthetic purposes; the family (like so many families both then and now) stylizes itself into patterns that promise both value and continuity.

As we have repeatedly seen, part I initiates a mode and form of argument that pervades the novel's aesthetic architecture. Because we discover the symbolic import of the Mengstrasse house at the same time the guests assembled for the housewarming do, we, in a wonderfully subtle way (the essential narrative gesture is reminiscent of Fontane's urbane eavesdropping), take part in the making of that symbol. We move into the novel just after the family moves into the house. Certain things are explained to us; others are not. And that mixture of explication and nonexplication is entirely appropriate to the working of the symbol. Any symbol must have an integrity of physical existence; the house certainly has that. The symbol also resonates with implications that are more than those of sheer factual identity; at every turn we sense that the house contains and speaks of a way of life in which family and firm constitute a powerful nexus of values. The symbol in literature both reveals and conceals; it is part of the felt complexity of human living whereby the interplay of physical thereness and spiritual signification is one of intense interaction. The spiritual meaning is both made physically intelligible and also hidden in the material form; the physicality is made transparent on the spiritual intimation but also conceals it. The symbol, then, has its truth in an interplay of revelation and concealment at one and the same time. This is superbly achieved by the exposition of *Buddenbrooks;* we, the readers, are party to the complex allusiveness of a way of life (and of the work of art that conveys that way of life).

The house is only one of many symbols inaugurated in part I. As part of the celebration of the new house, the town poet Jean Jacques Hoffstede recites a poem in honor of the family. The text of that poem finds its way into the collection of papers that makes up the family chronicle. At the beginning of part II we look over Jean's shoulder as he enters the birth of Clara into the chronicle and then browses through the pages, papers, letters, and so on. Gotthold's angry letters are there, as is Hoffstede's poem. Much later, when there is the occasion to celebrate a double engagement (Clara's to Pastor Tiburtius and Thomas's to Gerda), Tony will read out a stanza from Hoffstede's poem. When Tony grieves over the selling of the Mengstrasse house, she recalls the housewarming celebration—and Hoffstede's poem, which she knows by heart. With respect to this particular symbol, we, as readers, are present at the birth and maintenance of one particular emblem of family glory.

Many of the symbolic details are linguistic, and much has been written in the critical literature about Thomas Mann's fondness for leitmotivs.[2] No reader of *Buddenbrooks* can fail to notice them. But what scholarly invocations of either Homeric epithets or the role played by leitmotivs in Wagner's music dramas[3] tend to obscure is that the main justification for the frequency of leitmotivs in *Buddenbrooks* is thematic and realistic. The novel chronicles lives that are constantly anchored in the need to stylize experience into recurring rituals. The novel is also about change, about the decline of a family and the way of life it enshrines. Hence, the leitmotivs often articulate both the will to sameness and the ineluctable fact of difference and change. The individual Buddenbrooks so internalize this need for continuity that they often, we feel, do not fully realize what they are doing when they repeat themselves (and each other). Tony speaks both in the leitmotivs of family honor—"keeping up appearances," "distinguished," and so on—and in phrases that derive from her brief love affair with Morten Schwarzkopf, an affair that is crushed in the name of family continuity. Thomas borrows Christian's phrase about "lying low." Even experiences, it seems, are handed on; Tony gives up Morten, Thomas gives up Anna. Tony, Hanno, and Thomas all experience visits of particular poignancy to Travemünde. These symbolizations of the Buddenbrook way of life occasionally provide instances of a mismatch between the values by which the characters claim or seek to live and the deeds, objects, or phrases that are meant to enshrine those values.[4]

Even as early as part I there is an illustration—admittedly very harmless—of such a mismatch. At the housewarming, Dr. Grabow finds himself contemplating a prodigious display of bread, cakes, and salt cellars. The passage makes it clear that these objects partake of a traditional pair of symbolic gifts—salt and bread—that are given on the occasion of the entry into a new house. But as everybody associated with the Buddenbrooks is by definition a person of position, the bread and salt have to be transmuted into more grandiose, and expensive, physical emblems: "This was the 'Salt and Bread' that had been sent to the family by relatives or friends on the occasion of their moving house. But as one was supposed to see that the gifts did not come from lesser houses, the bread consisted of sweet, spicy, heavy confectionery, and the salt was housed in massive gold" (I, 2, 10). The note of disturbance is, of course, minimal; indeed, the only danger the family doctor registers is that of overeating. But the sense of something that has functional as well as spiritual integrity (both salt and bread are primary, and therefore useful, contributions to the larder as well as being gifts) being converted into mere show, into indicators of wealth, foreshadows what is to come and the crisis of symbolization that will express it.

The Family and Its Symbols

It is one of the bitter ironies of the decline of Thomas Budden-brook that he who prides himself on his intelligence and self-consciousness, on seeing the things of this world as having both the seriousness and the unseriousness of symbolic value, should increasingly succumb to the condition of being all representation and no substance. Part X begins with an extended narrative discussion of the increasing debility of Thomas, given precisely in terms of his weakening hold on his consciously self-symbolizing way of life: "To work playfully and to play with his work, to strive now with half-serious, now with half-joking, ambition for goals that one invests with only symbolic value—such serenely skeptical compromises and witty half-heartedness demand much freshness, humor, and good cheer; but Thomas Buddenbrook felt unspeakably weary and irritated" (X, 1, 477). Thomas, according to the bitter witticism of a business competitor, ends up living not complexly the complexity of symbolic existence but as a mere showman. His role at the stock exchange is "largely decorative" (478).

Thomas in his coffin is surrounded by the grandiose symbols of *haut-bourgeois* grief and condolence. As we read the narrator's description of the wreaths that pour into the house, we recall Dr. Grabow and the salt and the bread: "What one first of all had to do in this matter was to send wreaths, large wreaths, expensive wreaths, wreaths that redounded to one's own credit, which would be mentioned in the newspaper articles and from which it was entirely clear that they had been sent by upright and well-to-do people" (X, 9, 538). In the midst of all this symbolic overstatement, the strangled grief of Anna, Frau Iwersen, is wonderfully moving in its simple truth.

Hanno, of course, is even more oppressed by the symbols of Buddenbrook heritage than his father is. It is significant that one of his supreme symbolic gestures, a gesture in which physical deed and spiritual import are in perfect conjunction, is a devastating negation of the very storehouse of Buddenbrook symbols. He draws a double line across the family chronicle, under his own name, and explains that gesture to his outraged father with the words: "I thought . . . I thought . . . there was nothing more to come" (VIII, 7, 411).

13

Conclusion:
Symbolic Realism

Buddenbrooks is a thoughtful novel—and a novel about the coming
into being of thoughtfulness within a family. That thoughtfulness is
deployed not as validation of some privileged inwardness and spirituality but in order to show how mental life is unremittingly implicated in outward, practical, social affairs. The inwardness interlocks
with a rich picture of nineteenth-century social and familial life. It is
not only Tony who, in one of her favorite phrases, "keeps up appearances"; the novel does so too, while also tracing the complex needs
and promptings of the inner life. And that inner life is shown to be
not an intact realm of hermetic privacy but historicized in the sense
that it is part of the story and the history that Mann recounts. *Buddenbrooks* is full of dates; almost in the style of the family chronicle
that is so central to the tradition of the family of which it tells, the
text constantly gives precise indications of month and year.

In the context of European prose between about 1890 and 1920,
Buddenbrooks is one of many novels about family life. One of the
best-known to English-speaking readers is John Galsworthy's *The Forsyte Saga* (1906–1921). In the first volume of that novel sequence,
Soames Forsyte, the "man of property," comes to learn that there are

limits to his ability to own things—and people—and he loses his wife, Irene, to the architect Bosinney. Galsworthy clearly does perceive the interplay of outward (social) and inward (psychological) value scales, but he does not bring us close to the conceptual implications of that inner life in the way that Mann does.

A similar distinction obtains between Mann's novel and Max Kretzer's *Meister Timpe* of 1888. Kretzer's novel also registers the interplay in the family consciousness (and conscience) of private and public concerns. Timpe the craftsman-turner is gradually driven out of business by the mass-produced goods of the new factory, and his son Franz completes his downfall not only by working for the factory owner but also by stealing his father's treasured templates and making them available to the factory production lines. Kretzer is explicit in indicating the representative status of the two generations, and in the apportionment of his sympathy: "His son represented the new generation of the early Wilhelmine years, which was only concerned to earn easy money and to sacrifice the customs of the honest bourgeoisie to the Moloch of pleasure."[1] The novel leaves us in no doubt that the destruction of the father's livelihood and values is inevitable, and in the process the guild ethos will be destroyed, with its "lovely custom for the journeyman to have food and lodging in the house of his employer and thereby to be accounted one of the family."[2] As in *Buddenbrooks*, the "whole house" is the symbol of a way of life that is inexorably eroded by the currents of modern socioeconomic life.

There is much that is fine in Kretzer's work, as there is in Galsworthy's. But neither of them—nor Jonas Lie or Alexander Kielland whose family novels of the 1880s had a considerable influence on the young Thomas Mann—explores the subterranean connections between psychology (understood as both emotional and intellectual inwardness) and socioeconomic change with Mann's density of implication. It is not in spite of but because of its handling of the inner life that *Buddenbrooks*, paradoxically, is able so richly to comprehend the outer life. It is because of, and not in spite of, its artistic patterning that *Buddenbrooks* has so much more to say about the patterns of social and economic life than do Galsworthy or Kretzer.

In this study I have constantly insisted on the symbolic density of the *Buddenbrook* text. I want, by way of conclusion, to ask what the effect is on us the readers of this well-nigh claustrophobic intensity and insistence of patterned, symbolic statement.[3] Part of our response must be to see these symbols as anything but poeticizing or enabling devices; rather, they bespeak the characters' imprisoned condition. There is often a compulsive sameness to the characters' behavior (linguistic and other), and the patterns articulate either the characters' will to lead stylized, ritualized lives or the inexorable process of decline from which there is no escape. Either way, the characters emerge, at one level, as programmed creatures leading programmed lives. In this sense, *Buddenbrooks* belongs in the ambience of the European movement called naturalism, which came to the fore at the end of the nineteenth century. Naturalism derives from a sustained concern on the part of writers and thinkers to see human life under its scientific (and deterministic) aspect. Zola, Hauptmann, and Ibsen were all, in part at any rate, concerned to illuminate the knowable laws (of, for example, social or genetic conditioning) that act on human experience.

Yet *Buddenbrooks,* like all the greatest works of the period, is not content simply to demonstrate the law-driven predictability of human behavior. Many of its recurrent situations—the visits to Travemünde, Tony's phrases borrowed from Morten Schwarzkopf, Thomas's recurring perception of the brutal mechanism of life—affect us as something more than merely compulsive expressions of programmed living by programmed creatures. In these patterns we discern a selfhood trying to cope with disturbing, problematic experience. There may be no way out for any of the characters, but the pain is still proof that the self is not totally conditioned, not functioning on automatic pilot. There is still a measure of dignity left to the characters, a dignity inseparable from their sense of deprivation and from their struggle (however unsuccessful) to understand themselves—perhaps even to liberate themselves.

Tony is a good example of what I mean. She is, by any standards, a "programmed" Buddenbrook. And her formulaic phrases are, in countless ways, symptomatic of a life entirely contained within the imposed (and self-imposed) limits of obedience to an ethos that is never far from her mind. Yet some of her formulaic repetitions—and I think particularly of the phrases she derives from Morten about, for example, "sitting on the stones" or "knowing what you are getting with honey"—obstinately vibrate with the memory of a glimpse of human fulfillment, irrevocably forfeited. I have no wish to sentimentalize this figure, not least because the novel is so wonderfully unsentimental about her. Tony's phrasemaking is the measure of her mindlessness; she can make even the experience with Morten yield a set of serviceable clichés. Yet behind the clichés we still hear, obstinately present, a selfhood that constantly recalls the time with Morten as part of a private code to which no one else is party. For me there is a significant difference between her parrotting a phrase such as "keeping up appearances" and the phrases that come from Morten. Those phrases keep alive, however vestigially, a corner of inwardness in her that is not simply aligned with the Buddenbrook ethos. Hence it is she who understands better than anybody else in the family Hanno's heartbreak at having to leave Travemünde. She comforts him with a story she told Morten in the early days of their love: how, when she was little, she took a large number of jellyfish home in her handkerchief, hoping that, as the water evaporated, the stars would be left behind. But the end result was a damp patch on the balcony—"it only smelt a bit of rotten seaweed" (III, 8, 105; X, 4, 500). The echo is touching and beautiful, and the symbolic resonance of the little anecdote—to the effect that the freedom and beauty of life at Travemünde cannot be transported back to Lübeck—speaks eloquently of deprivation deeply felt. In such moments we still hear and are hurt by the moral outrage done to Tony's love by the commercial imperatives of the Buddenbrook ethos.

Many of the symbols to which I have drawn attention work with this complex dialectic whereby they express both regimented thought and behavior patterns and also the vulnerability trapped within that regimentation. In an entirely precise distillation of sociopsychological mechanisms, the symbols both reveal and conceal, both acknowledge and repress, both articulate and regiment socially problematic human feelings. And we the readers register the patterns with the perception made available to us by the novel's marvelously intricate structure, a perception that acknowledges both the determinism and the dignity of the human condition. Thomas Mann at one point responded very sternly to a reader who saw in *Buddenbrooks* only precisely recorded social experience: "I was, however, very surprised that you 'looked in vain' in my novel for the 'exceptional,' the 'transcendental.' What of the music? What of Thomas Buddenbrook's adventure with Schopenhauer? Am I really only a depicter of good lunches?"[4]

Buddenbrooks looks back on the whole legacy of European realism and naturalism from the late eighteenth century on through the nineteenth century. Both artistic tendencies have to do with the growth of science—the science of nature and the science of society—as it emerged in the hundred or so years prior to the publication of *Buddenbrooks*. Notions of scientific law entail notions of determinism, yet so many of the great writers from this tradition also look, in their fictions, for the small areas of exemption, of nondetermined knowing and feeling, that are the repository of humanity. *Buddenbrooks* is wonderfully true to this complex legacy and ultimately reflects on it precisely in the sense that certain of the characters come, by implication, to reflect on it. In so doing they stand outside their own existences as realistic-cum-naturalistic characters in a realistic-cum-naturalistic novel. But such moments of privileged, and devastating, inwardness do not help them to break free of the kind of living in which they have grown up, of the kind of novel fiction appropriate to their conditioning. Yet some of the characters have the dignity of questioning, even, perhaps, of questing. For this reason *Buddenbrooks* manages to see the inner life both as symptomatic of the age in which it exists (determined in that sense) and as sometimes possessing, against all the odds, the dignity of suffering from the determined condition. Mann suggested something of this when he wrote,

> We were caught halfway between the limitless expansion of the industrial "boom years" and the World War, which was to announce the end of the bourgeois age. The fathers had achieved everything,

we were inheritors, we already felt the great tiredness of the end. . . .
This historical motif in my book was everywhere registered simul-
taneously. . . . That the author set mind and body in a certain con-
tradiction, that he saw mind as the product of a process of
biological decline, all that tallied with the prevailing mood without
succumbing slavishly to it in its rigid commitment to *social*
determinism.[5]

At the end of Ibsen's *Ghosts,* the genetic, determining argument
about human destiny runs its appointed course, and Oswald's mind is
invaded by the disease he knew had to destroy him sooner or later.
When his mind goes, he does not, however, simply utter incoherent
babble. He repeats over and over again what is at one level a childish
refrain and at another an assertion of the dignity of the suffering self
that longs for better, righter, truer human living. "Give me the sun,"
he says. In this amazing symbolic end to the play, Ibsen holds in focus,
in simultaneous truthfulness, both a lacerating image of human im-
prisonment and a poetic cry for better than caged living. *Buddenbrooks,* too, achieves this wonder of human and aesthetic balance in
its constantly reverberating symbols.

Rilke, in the fourth of his *Duino Elegies,* laments the imperfect
cognition from which we of the modern, disinherited age suffer: "We
do not know the contour / Of feeling: only what forms it from outside."[6] Rilke may perhaps have in mind here the consequences—or, as
he would see them, the deprivations—brought about by a century or
so of European realism with its weighty concentration on the outward
formings and deformings of our inner life by the material world.
Thomas Mann's *Buddenbrooks* shows us abundantly the things that
"form the feeling from outside," and it is in this sense one of the tow-
ering achievements of European realism. But Mann shows us not just
the outward envelope of feeling but also the inner space of human
feeling. *Pace* Rilke, he gives us the feeling from inside; he finds words
and even concepts for it. He shows the inward life as contoured by the
pressures from outside, as delimited by those contours, as therefore
imprinted by the outside world, but he also upholds that inward life

as the guarantor of human striving for truer understanding, truer living. Small wonder, then, that Rilke was one of the first, and most profoundly appreciative, readers of *Buddenbrooks*. Small wonder that *Buddenbrooks* has continued to find generation after generation of appreciative readers.

NOTES

For works cited fully in the Selected Bibliography, I give only an abbreviated reference.

Chronology

1. Quoted in Paul Scherrer, "Bruchstücke der *Buddenbrooks*-Urhandschrift," 258.

2. "Lübeck als geistige Lebensform," in Thomas Mann, *Das essayistische Werk*, ed. Hans Bürgin, *Autobiographisches* (Frankfurt: Fischer Bücherei, 1968), 180.

3. See T. J. Reed's admirable discussion of the genesis of the novel as a process whereby a precocious and ironic talent acquires a substantial theme, in *Thomas Mann: The Uses of Tradition*, 80–85.

4. See Julia Mann, "Tante Elisabeth," *Sinn und Form*, 15 (1963): 482–96.

5. See Uwe Ebel, *Rezeption und Integration*, 153–60.

6. See Ken Moulden and Gero von Wilpert, eds., *Buddenbrooks-Handbuch*, 11 ff.

7. Ulrich Dietzel, ed., "Aus den Familienpapieren," 37. See also Fritz Hofmann, *"Buddenbrooks,"* 33.

8. Ebel, 37.

9. On the genesis of the novel, see Mann's own essays "Bilse und ich," *Betrachtungen eines Unpolitischen*, and "Lübeck als geistige Lebensform," and the studies by Peter de Mendelssohn, Hofmann, Moulden and Wilpert, and Scherrer listed in the Selected Bibliography.

10. See Martin Swales, "In Defence of Weimar: Thomas Mann and the Politics of Republicanism," in *Weimar Germany: Writers and Politics*, ed. A. F. Bance (St. Andrews: Scottish Academic Press, 1982), 1–13.

1. The German Background

1. Reed is surely right to insist (*Thomas Mann: The Uses of Tradition,* 40ff. and passim) on the novelistic skill with which both real-life material and ideas are woven into the texture of the narrative.

2. Hans Wysling, ed., *Thomas Mann: Dichter über ihre Dichtungen,* 48.

3. "Lübeck als geistige Lebensform," in *Das essayistische Werk, Autobiographisches,* 183.

4. See, for example, Wolfgang Preisendanz, *Wege des Realismus* (Munich: Fink, 1977), and Klaus-Detlef Müller, ed., *Bürgerlicher Realismus* (Königstein: Athenäum, 1981).

5. See Hartmut Steinecke, ed., *Romanpoetik in Deutschland* (Tübingen: Narr, 1984), and Gerhard Plumpe, ed., *Theorie des bürgerlichen Realismus* (Stuttgart: Reclam, 1985).

6. See Arthur C. Danto, *Analytical Philosophy of History* (Cambridge: Cambridge University Press, 1985); Hayden White, *Metahistory* (Baltimore and London: Johns Hopkins University Press, 1973); Paul Ricoeur, *Time and Narrative,* trans: K. McLaughlin and D. Pellauer (Chicago and London: Chicago University Press, 1984).

7. See especially Ian Watt, *The Rise of the Novel* (Harmondsworth: Penguin, 1963), and Raymond Williams, *The English Novel from Dickens to Lawrence* (St. Albans: Paladin, 1974).

8. David Blackbourn and Geoff Eley, *The Peculiarities of German History* (Oxford: Oxford University Press, 1984); see also Wolfgang J. Mommsen, *Britain and Germany 1800 to 1914: Two Developmental Paths towards Industrial Society* (London: German Historical Institute, 1986).

9. Mack Walker, *German Home Towns* (Ithaca, N.Y. and London: Cornell University Press, 1971).

10. Raymond Williams, *The Country and the City* (St. Albans: Paladin, 1975).

11. See "The Natural History of German Life," *Westminster Review* 66 (July 1856): 51–76.

12. See Timothy McFarland, "Wagner's Nuremberg," in Nicholas John, ed., *Richard Wagner: "The Mastersingers of Nuremberg,"* English National Opera Guides, 19 (London: English National Opera, 1983), 27–34.

2. *Buddenbrooks* and European Realism

1. See Christopher Prendergast, *The Order of Mimesis* (Cambridge: Cambridge University Press, 1986).

Notes

3. Critical Reception

1. See the helpful survey of the reception history of *Buddenbrooks* in Moulden and Wilpert, eds., *Buddenbrooks-Handbuch*, 319ff.

2. Inge Diersen, *Untersuchungen zu Thomas Mann;* Georg Lukács, *Thomas Mann;* Hans Mayer, *Thomas Mann.*

3. See especially the compilation in Klaus Schröter, ed., *Thomas Mann im Urteil seiner Zeit*, and Rudolf Wolff, ed., *Thomas Manns "Buddenbrooks" und die Wirkung.*

4. See Manfred Jurgensen's contribution to Moulden and Wilpert, eds., *Buddenbrooks-Handbuch,* esp. 126; Helmut Koopmann, *Die Entwicklung des "intellektualen Romans" bei Thomas Mann;* Herbert Lehnert, *Thomas Mann: Fiktion—Mythos—Religion;* Peter Pütz, "Die Stufen des Bewusstseins"; Klaus-Jürgen Rothenberg, *Das Problem des Realismus bei Thomas Mann.*

5. *Thomas Mann: Epoche, Werk, Wirkung,* 81.

4. A "loose baggy monster"?

1. Roland Barthes, "L'Effet du réel," *Communications* 11 (1968): 84–89, and J. P. Stern, *On Realism* (London: Routledge & Kegan Paul, 1973), 5.

2. Henry James, Preface to *The Tragic Muse* in *The Novels and Tales of Henry James,* New York Edition, vol. 7 (New York: Scribner, 1936), x. See Barbara Hardy's discussion of James's remark in *The Appropriate Form: An Essay on the Novel* (London: Athlone, 1971), 3–7.

3. See Lilian Furst's paper, "Re-reading *Buddenbrooks,*" forthcoming in *German Life and Letters.*

4. For a contrasting view, see Patricia Drechsel Tobin, *Time and the Novel: The Genealogical Imperative* (Princeton, N.J.: Princeton University Press, 1978), 69.

5. See Luise Liefländer-Koistinen, *Zu Thomas Manns "Buddenbrooks,"* 3–5.

6. See, for example, the studies by Eckhard Heftrich, Erich Heller, and Peter Pütz.

7. See Eberhard Lämmert, "Thomas Mann: *Buddenbrooks,*" esp. 205. For helpful observations on the psychological (as opposed to the philosophical) issue, see L. D. Nachman and A. S. Braverman, "Thomas Mann's *Buddenbrooks.*"

8. Henry James, "The Art of Fiction" in *The Future of the Novel: Essays on the Art of Fiction,* ed. Leon Edel (New York: Vintage Books, 1956), 14.

9. I am deeply indebted to Jochen Vogt's superb discussion of the exposition in *Thomas Mann: "Buddenbrooks,"* 13–28.

5. Family Occasions

1. Hofmann, 33.

2. See Vogt's admirable discussion of W. H. Riehl in *Thomas Mann,* 31ff.

3. Thomas Mann, "Der alte Fontane," *Das essayistische Werk,* ed. Hans Bürgin, *Schriften und Reden zur Literatur, Kunst, und Philosophie,* vol. 1 (Frankfurt: Fischer Bücherei, 1968), 48.

4. See Ebel, 45–50, and Vogt, 15–18.

6. Psychology and Character Drawing

1. *Thomas Mann (Dichter über ihre Dichtungen),* 51.

2. See Hugh Ridley's splendid discussion of this scene in *Thomas Mann: "Buddenbrooks,"* 38–55. For an analysis of the Nietzschean implications of the antagonism between the brothers, see Hans Rudolf Vaget, "Der Asket und der Komödiant."

7. Narrative Technique: Temporal and Spatial Specifications

1. Lilian Furst, "Realism and Its Codes of Accreditation," *Comparative Literature Studies* 25 (1988): 101–26, and see her forthcoming "Re-reading *Buddenbrooks.*"

2. Furst, "Realism and Its Codes of Accreditation," 116.

3. See Bernd W. Seiler, "Ironischer Stil und realistischer Eindruck."

8. Narrative Technique: The Inner Realm

1. See Roy Pascal, *The Dual Voice* (Manchester: Manchester University Press, 1977).

9. Inwardness

1. See Heftrich's thoughtful discussion of this figure in *Vom Verfall zur Apokalypse,* 47ff.

2. *Thomas Mann: Dichter über ihre Dichtungen,* 98.

3. Ibid., 49.

4. Ibid., 98.

Notes

5. F. R. Leavis, "*Hard Times,* an Analytic Note," in *The Great Tradition* (Harmondsworth: Penguin, 1966), 249–56.

6. See the discussion of the beginning and the end of the novel offered by Lämmert, Lehnert, and Vogt.

7. See Pierre-Paul Sagave, *Réalité sociale et idéologie religieuse.*

8. Max Weber, *The Protestant Ethic and the Spirit of Capitalism* (London: George Allen & Unwin, 1985), and R. H. Tawney, *Religion and the Rise of Capitalism* (Harmondsworth: Penguin, 1985).

9. *Thomas Mann: Dichter über ihre Dichtungen,* 54.

10. Music

1. See the discussion of Wagner by Erwin Koppen in Hermann Kurzke, ed., *Stationen der Thomas-Mann-Forschung,* 228–46.

2. See Ebel, 44–46.

11. Of Economic Signs and Symbols

1. See note 8 to chapter 4.

2. Gustav Lindtke, *Die Stadt der Buddenbrooks,* 13.

3. *Thomas Mann: Dichter über ihre Dichtungen,* 54.

4. See Kurzke, *Thomas Mann,* 49–50; Moulden and Wilpert, 196, 254; Vogt, 69; Michael Zeller, *Bürger oder Bourgeois?,* 22–29.

5. *Thomas Mann: Dichter über ihre Dichtungen,* 54.

6. See Ernst Wolf's discussion of the Hagenströms' role as components of the Buddenbrook sociopsychology ("Hagenströms: The Rival Family").

7. Vogt, 76–80.

8. On the economic representativeness of the feckless husbands, see Zeller, *Väter und Söhne.*

9. See Pierre-Paul Sagave, "Zur Geschichtlichkeit von Thomas Manns Jugendroman."

10. See Otto Brunner, "Das ganze Haus," in *Neue Wege der Verfassungs- und Sozialgeschichte* (Göttingen: Vandenhoeck und Ruprecht, 1968), and Vogt, 29–39.

11. *Thomas Mann: Dichter über ihre Dichtungen,* 53.

12. "Lübeck als geistige Lebensform," in *Das essayistische Werk, Autobiographisches,* 186.

13. On this point I find myself in disagreement with Kurzke, Ridley, and Vogt, all of whom attribute a dimension of socioeconomic understanding to the novel—only then to withdraw it.

12. The Family and Its Symbols

1. Lämmert, esp. 223ff., insists on the extent to which the aesthetic patterns are expressive of sociological patterns.

2. One of the earliest—and still one of the best—studies is Ronald Peacock's *Das Leitmotiv bei Thomas Mann*. On the repetitions and their interlocking function, see Koopmann, *Die Entwicklung des "intellektualen Romans."*

3. See Vaget's "Thomas Mann und Wagner."

4. See Gunter Reiss, *Allegorisierung,* esp. 65–69.

13. Conclusion: Symbolic Realism

1. I quote here my own translation from Max Kretzer, *Meister Timpe* (Stuttgart: Reclam, 1976), 20–21.

2. *Meister Timpe,* 66–67.

3. See Christoph Geiser, *Naturalismus und Symbolismus,* 35.

4. *Thomas Mann: Dichter über ihre Dichtungen,* 39.

5. Ibid., 106.

6. Rainer Maria Rilke, *Duineser Elegien* in *Sämtliche Werke,* ed. Ernst Zinn, vol. 1, *Gedichte: erster Teil* (Frankfurt: Insel, 1955), 697.

SELECTED BIBLIOGRAPHY

Primary Works

Buddenbrooks. Translated by Helen T. Lowe-Porter. New York: Alfred A. Knopf, 1924.

Gesammelte Werke in dreizehn Bänden. Frankfurt: Fischer, 1974.

Thomas Mann (Dichter über ihre Dichtungen). Vol. 14. Compiled by Hans Wysling and Marianne Fischer. Frankfurt: Heimeran/Fischer, 1975.

Secondary Works

Background

Dietzel, Ulrich, and Gerda Weissenfels, eds. Aus den Familienpapieren der Manns: Dokumente zu den "Buddenbrooks." Berlin: Aufbau, 1965.

Mann, Julia. "Tante Elisabeth." Sinn und Form 15 (1963): 482–96.

Scherrer, Paul. "Aus Thomas Manns Vorapbeiten zu den Buddenbrooks: Zur Chronologie des Romans." In Quellenkritische Studien zum Werk Thomas Manns, vol. 1, edited by Paul Scherrer and Hans Wysling. Bern and Munich: Francke, 1967.

———. "Bruchstücke der Buddenbrooks-Urhandschrift." Neue Rundschau (1958): 258–91.

Biography

Hamilton, Nigel. The Brothers Mann: The Lives of Heinrich and Thomas Mann. London: Secker & Warburg, 1978.

Mendelssohn, Peter de. *Der Zauberer: Das Leben des deutschen Schriftstellers Thomas Mann.* Vol. 1 Frankfurt: Fischer, 1975.

Winston, Richard. *Thomas Mann: The Making of an Artist.* London: Constable, 1982.

Criticism: Books

Diersen, Inge. *Untersuchungen zu Thomas Mann.* Berlin: Rütten und Loening, 1965. Stresses the social and realistic import of the novel.

Ebel, Uwe. *Rezeption und Integration skandinavischer Literatur in Thomas Manns "Buddenbrooks."* Neumünster: Wachholtz, 1974. A very full study of Mann's indebtedness to Scandinavian literary sources.

Geiser, Christoph. *Naturalismus und Symbolismus im Frühwerk Thomas Manns.* Bern and Munich: Francke, 1971. Good on the interplay of "aesthetic" and "scientific" strategies.

Hansen, Volkmar. *Thomas Mann.* Stuttgart: Metzler, 1984. Provides a helpful introduction and bibliography.

Heftrich, Eckhard. *Vom Verfall zur Apokalypse: Über Thomas Mann.* Vol. 2. Frankfurt: Klostermann, 1982. Idiosyncratic study of character, with some helpful insights.

Heller, Erich. *Thomas Mann: The Ironic German.* Cambridge: Cambridge University Press, 1979. Still a splendidly eloquent reading of the novel in philosophical terms.

Koopmann, Helmut. *Die Entwicklung des "intellektualen Romans" bei Thomas Mann.* Bonn: Bouvier, 1980. Very acute in its tracing of cross-references and patternings in the text.

Kurzke, Hermann, ed. *Stationen der Thomas-Mann-Forschung: Aufsätze seit 1970.* Würzburg: Königshausen und Neumann, 1985. Thoughtful essays on particular aspects.

———. *Thomas Mann: Epoche, Werk, Wirkung.* Munich: Beck, 1985. Superb literature survey, coupled with Kurzke's own perceptive commentary on the novel.

Lehnert, Herbert. *Thomas Mann: Fiktion—Mythos—Religion.* Stuttgart: Kohlhammer, 1965. Stresses the novel as an aesthetic (rather than realistic) statement.

Liefländer-Koistinen, Luise. *Zu Thomas Manns "Buddenbrooks": Einige Überlegungen zur Darstellung und Funktion der Figur Tony Buddenbrook.* Oulu, Finland: Universität Oulu, 1980. Careful study of Tony.

Lindtke, Gustav. *Die Stadt der Buddenbrooks: Lübecker Bürgerkultur im 19.*

Selected Bibliography

Jahrhundert. Lübeck: Schmidt-Römhild, 1965. Informative study of Lübeck in the nineteenth century.

Lukács, Georg. *Thomas Mann.* Berlin: Aufbau, 1957. Originally published in 1949, Lukács's study is still important for the sociocultural implications of the novel.

Mayer, Hans. *Thomas Mann.* Frankfurt: Suhrkamp, 1980. A recently revised version of an important study of the social aspects of the novel.

Moulden, Ken, and Gero von Wilpert, eds. *Buddenbrooks-Handbuch.* Stuttgart: Kröner, 1988. Very full treatment of different aspects of the novel.

Peacock, Ronald. *Das Leitmotiv bei Thomas Mann.* Bern: Haupt, 1934. Still very useful as a survey of the leitmotivs.

Reed, T. J. *Thomas Mann: The Uses of Tradition.* Oxford: Clarendon, 1974. A splendid study, particularly impressive on the genesis of the novel and on its sheer narrative power.

Reiss, Gunter. *Allegorisierung und moderne Erzählkunst: Eine Studie zum Werk Thomas Manns.* Munich: Fink, 1970. Thoughtful in its argument about the links between social change and narrative modes.

Ridley, Hugh. *Thomas Mann: "Buddenbrooks."* Cambridge: Cambridge University Press, 1987. A judicious and thoughtful introduction to the novel.

Rothenberg, Klaus-Jürgen. *Das Problem des Realismus bei Thomas Mann: Zur Behandlung von Wirklichkeit in den "Buddenbrooks."* Cologne and Vienna: Böhlau, 1969. Insists on the novel as an aestheticization (rather than a realistic depiction) of social and family life.

Sagave, Pierre-Paul. *Realité sociale et idéologie religieuse dans les romans de Thomas Mann.* Paris: Société d'Edition Les Belles Lettres, 1954. Splendidly acute on the interplay of religious and economic themes.

Schröter, Klaus, ed. *Thomas Mann im Urteil seiner Zeit.* Hamburg: Wegner, 1969. Excellent compilation of responses to Mann's literary production.

Vogt, Jochen. *Thomas Mann: "Buddenbrooks."* Munich: Fink, 1983. A first-rate study, summarizing the scholarly literature to date, but also adding important new perspectives.

Wolff, Rudolf, ed. *Thomas Manns "Buddenbrooks" und die Wirkung.* 2 vols. Bonn: Bouvier, 1986. Helpful compilation of the novel's critical reception.

Zeller, Michael. *Bürger oder Bourgeois? Eine literatursoziologische Studie zu Thomas Manns "Buddenbrooks" und Heinrich Manns "Im Schlaraffen-land."* Stuttgart: Klett, 1976. An energetic study of the extent (and the limitations) of *Buddenbrooks* as a chronicle of social and economic change.

—————. *Väter und Söhne bei Thomas Mann.* Bonn: Bouvier, 1974. Suggestive pointers to the links between the family and processes of social change.

Criticism: Articles

Hofmann, Fritz. *"Buddenbrooks: Verfall einer Familie."* In *Das erzählerische Werk Thomas Manns,* ed. Klaus Hermsdorf, 9–59. Berlin: Aufbau, 1976. A splendid survey of the sources of the novel and of their implications for its interpretation.

Kolb, Jocelyne. "Thomas Mann's Translation of Wagner into *Buddenbrooks.*" *Germanic Review* 61 (1986): 146–53. Good discussion of the associative richness of the leitmotivs.

Lämmert, Eberhard. "Thomas Mann: *Buddenbrooks.*" In *Der deutsche Roman: Vom Barock bis zur Gegenwart,* ed. Benno von Wiese, vol. 2, 190–233. Düsseldorf: Bagel, 1963. Superb study of the novel.

Lehnert, Herbert. *"Buddenbrooks."* In *Deutsche Romane des 20. Jahrhunderts: Neue Interpretationen,* ed. Paul Michael Lützeler, 31–49. Königstein: Athenäum, 1983. Good on the implications of the religious issue.

Nachman, L. D., and A. S. Braverman. "Thomas Mann's *Buddenbrooks:* Bourgeois Society and the Inner Life." *Germanic Review* 45 (1970): 201–25. Good on the psychological processes in the novel.

Pütz, Peter. "Die Stufen des Bewusstseins bei Schopenhauer und den Buddenbrooks." In *Teilnahme und Spiegelung* (Festschrift für Horst Rüdiger), ed. Beda Allemann and Erwin Koppen, 443–52. Berlin and New York: De Gruyter, 1975. Finely discriminating study of Schopenauerean patterns in the novel.

Sagave, Pierre-Paul. "Zur Geschichtlichkeit von Thomas Manns Jugendroman: Bürgerliches Klassenbewusstsein und kapitalistische Praxis in *Buddenbrooks.*" *Literaturwissenschaft und Geschichtsphilosophie* (Festschrift für W. Emrich), ed. Helmut Arntzen, 436–52. Berlin and New York: De Gruyter, 1975. Thoughtful on the relationships between Buddenbrook inwardness and socioeconomic praxis.

Seiler, Bernd W. "Ironischer Stil und realistischer Eindruck: Zu einem scheinbaren Widerspruch in der Erzählkunst Thomas Manns." *Deutsche Vierteljahrsschrift für Literaturwissenschaft und Geistesgeschichte* 60 (1986): 459–83. A very acute study of narrative tone.

Vaget, Hans Rudolf. "Der Asket und der Komödiant: die Brüder Buddenbrook." *Modern Language Notes* 97 (1982): 656–70. Nietzschean reading of the tension between Thomas and Christian.

———. "Thomas Mann und Wagner: Zur Funktion des Leitmotivs in *Der Ring des Nibelungen* und *Buddenbrooks.*" In *Literatur und Musik,* ed. Steven Paul Scher. Berlin: Schmidt, 1984. Thoughtful discussion of the architectonics of the leitmotivs.

Wolf, Ernst M. "Hagenströms: The Rival Family in Thomas Mann's *Buddenbrooks.*" *German Studies Review* 5 (1982): 35–55. Thoughtful discussion of the overlap and contrast between the Hagenströms and the Buddenbrooks.

INDEX

THE AUTHOR

Martin Swales, a native of Victoria, British Columbia, received his B.A. from the University of Cambridge in 1961 and his Ph.D. from the University of Birmingham in 1963. He has held teaching positions in German at the University of Birmingham; the University of Toronto; King's College, London; and University College, London, where he is professor and head of the German Department. His publications include *Arthur Schnitzler: A Critical Study* (1971), *The German Novelle* (1977), *The German Bildungsroman from Wieland to Hesse* (1978), *Thomas Mann* (1980), (with Erika Swales) *Adalbert Stifter: A Critical Study* (1984), and *Goethe's "The Sorrows of Young Werther"* (1987).